The Pulp Mindset

A NewPub Survival Guide

JD Cowan

D1570242

The Pulp Mindset

Welcome to NewPub

If you are in possession of this book it can be assumed that you are at least partially aware of the sea change currently occurring in the world of art. Big chain book stores are dying, ebooks are taking off, and major publishers are absorbing massive losses from both of the above. Fewer people in the modern world read than ever before; no one watches television or buys music much anymore, and Hollywood is hemorrhaging money from bomb after bomb. Things certainly look bleak for modern entertainment.

Despite this, the online space of new creators grows more with each passing day. These mavericks are snatching up what the dying industry is losing. Audiences still want entertainment, but not so much from the old guard. The twentieth century has finally been left behind, and the world is moving into a new age. You are living in a transitional period of art where anything goes.

New writers, however, are a bit lost at sea. Should they trust these old creaky corporate behemoths that are but a shadow of their former glory, or should they strike it out on their own in this burgeoning, yet confusing, landscape? It looks like a tough call, at first glance, but the answer is easier than it's ever been.

The old publishing world—"OldPub"—is dying.

What were once the Big Five major book publishers that ruled the West have contracted, and the large lumber industry feeding their giant bookstore chain is drying up. The days of acquiring a big book contract and having a hit bestseller topping the charts for weeks is over. In an era where no one buys from those Big Five publishers anymore, this is a pipe dream. A writer who chooses this dusty path is looking at a dead end with a limited future. This OldPub world is breathing its last breaths.

Meanwhile, the new publishing world—"NewPub"—is thriving. This is the online independent space that is only stealing more and more of the old guard's lunch with every passing day. While OldPub tumbles down the hill, the new blood pushes up instead.

Today, some authors make hundreds of thousands on their books without the interference of any publishing company. They do not have to relinquish an absurd cut of their profits to a publisher, either. What you can make in NewPub far outstrips what you could in the dinosaur industry. Others find niches for themselves, cranking out their works to a loyal audience that manages to steadily increase in number with each new release. The road ahead for new creators is rocky, but it can lead to much success with enough effort.

This NewPub world is the inevitable future of book publishing. The freedom offered here for both customer and creator is overwhelming. Ignore it at your own peril. Sadly, many new writers are.

Of course, there is still no guaranteed path to success, there never is with art, but there are more options to succeed in the wild west of NewPub than there is in the cold corporate fringes of OldPub. At the very least, you have full control over what you put out.

It goes without saying that if you are reading this then you are already either aware of the shift or curious enough to dig deeper into the subject. You want to see just what this fancy NewPub thing is all about and how to take advantage of it. Well, there are most likely a few reasons why you haven't done so yet.

NewPub has a problem. It is tied to the outdated advice of dinosaurs from decades ago, holding new writers back from fully taking advantage of the wide open opportunities before them. These dinosaurs are part of OldPub, still passing out the same bad guidance that led their own industry into the death throes it is currently in and preventing upcoming writers from succeeding in this new landscape. Did you catch that? Yes, that's right: what's holding back new creators from succeeding is advice from an old industry that is failing.

Much of this either comes from misplaced nostalgia or an outdated mindset. There is nothing OldPub can teach you in order to succeed in NewPub. The fact that new publishing is even thriving at all is partially due to the fact that the corporate behemoths are floundering as badly as they are. But many new writers still find themselves attracted to the bells and whistles of OldPub.

For instance, if you are a writer who still thinks getting an agent or having a publisher logo on the side of your book is the key to success, then you are a victim of this backwards thinking. You have the wrong mindset for a new writer to have. This book you are currently reading is precisely for upcoming creators like you. Your sabotaged and antiquated mindset will hold you back, and keep you from being the best you can be.

To move forward, writers need a new mindset: a mindset based on customer-first practices and a writing style that prioritizes entertainment above all. In the entertainment world there was once a time when creators thrived by putting entertainment first, and it is an era you need to seriously consider when becoming a writer yourself. You have to take your focus back to the early twentieth century, from before the mess OldPub is currently in, and learn from the true masters.

What you need is a pulp mindset.

This is a shift that requires looking to the past, long before the corporate minefield of OldPub became the lumbering, decaying mammoth it is today. You need to return to when writing was at its most prolific, wide-reaching, and exciting—all the antithesis of what the industry is today and what it champions. This means reconnecting with an unjustly-maligned past to construct a better future.

The pulps have suffered from much revisionism over the last century, mostly from those who have never read them or who take them out of context in order to prevent new readers from experiencing them at all. Understanding their success is invaluable in realizing just what has been lost over the years in modern writing, and what can be reclaimed.

When the pulps were around, everyone read. As they faded away and were replaced with fat, overwritten tomes about the drudgery of modern life, the audience walked away. Decades of this audience-repelling attitude has led to the current state of the industry. No one reads anymore because they think reading is about the garbage OldPub puts out. However, when the pulps were king this wasn't the case.

Literally every aspect of OldPub is as anti-pulp as it can get, and that is why it is currently failing. This is to your advantage. NewPub embracing pulp is their ace in the hole that will help them win over their stumbling competition.

This pulp mindset will change your way of thinking and allow you to write stories totally unlike anything OldPub is dishing out, with their dwindling sales and audience interest. A new exciting world exists ahead, unconstrained by the limits of their dying industry. This brand new frontier before you is going to be built on pulp. It is inevitable.

You can be a part of this new pulp landscape, and it won't take much at all. You only need to shift your way of thinking.

If you are not sure what being pulp entails, hold on, it will be addressed very shortly. First, some clarifications are needed.

Now, this book is not a How-To manual. It's not about gaming algorithms for online book sales or a formula to writing a top seller. There are few practical tips to tell: it's all about having a mental edge. This is a book about how to gain a mindset to survive as a new writer in the saloon shootout that is NewPub, and why you should ditch the boneyard that is OldPub. All that other material from writing formulas to book formatting to advertising comes after you have learned the pulp mindset.

First thing's first, make sure you approach this new frontier with the right attitude and that requires doing things you were told not to do for decades by writing courses, literature professors, and historical revisionists. Assess the past and appreciate what it can offer you. In order to be pulp, you need to understand what that entails. There is more to it than the over the top comic art you've seen parodied countless times over your life. It's also an attitude, and a writing style. You must put the audience first, and that is scary to modern writers!

Pulp is actually a good bit more dangerous than how "offensive" the art or language is. It breaks all the rules. You would be surprised to learn that pulp writers are far less limited than modern writers are because of their cavalier attitude towards creativity and craft. They could do anything, and they frequently did so.

Pulp writers in the first half of the twentieth century pumped out hundreds of thousands of words with no regard to genre or future political discourse. They concentrated on establishing awe, action, and clear moral stakes, and yet they had boundless imaginative ideas to prop it all up. What they did was put one rule forward: *the audience must be entertained above everything else.* Know your audience, and give them what they want before you throw a curve ball or whatever is that you wish to do. This is the key to the pulp mindset.

This sounds strange in an era of overbearing artist ego and fanatical worship of content makers, but it is paramount to changing the way you think about writing in this ever-shifting era. As stated earlier, the modern industry is completely anti-pulp and backwards, and that is why it is failing. In order to change that, you need to look for another way to progress past the muck of OldPub. You need to reclaim what was lost, and work forward from that.

The pulp path is the only way forward, and it is what NewPub can do better than anyone else. Remember: the dinosaurs are dying because they have abandoned what the audience wants. All you have to do is remember what they've forgotten, and apply it!

The audience and the artist exist together in order to work off each other, with the audience being the more important of the two. They pay, you deliver, and you both get what you want. It was once that simple. However, we live in a time where the audience wants more, and the artist offers less. How can this be reconciled?

You understand now. It is reconciled by looking back to a past long abandoned by the currently dying dinosaur industry and taking up what they have thrown away. It is about becoming a pulp writer and putting the audience first.

Yes, OldPub is dying, but you do not have to die with it. The solution to moving into the future lies in recovering a past you were told to avoid and dismiss without a second glance. You must do the opposite of what OldPub wants you to do.

The solution to the modern ails of upcoming writers involves gaining a pulp mindset, and marching into this dangerous NewPub world where anything can happen. This is what the book you are now reading exists to help you do. Read on and you will soon find yourself equipped with the pulp mindset you need to survive.

Welcome to the new world. You have quite the journey ahead of you.

What is Pulp?

To understand why those ancient pulps are worth looking over, it is important to remember where they came from. In order to move towards the future, one must understand their past. So it only makes sense to start there.

Before World War II the most common form of entertainment was reading. Movies were costly and only available to watch once in the theater, and television was fairly limited at its outset, with only a miniscule number of programs and no way to record them. Other than radio (which, again, ran on a tight schedule), reading was the most accessible type of entertainment available for the cheapest possible price. Anyone could walk into a library, and anyone could spend a dime on a magazine. They were the only form of entertainment that could be taken and enjoyed everywhere.

And the audiences took full advantage.

Pulp magazines were where readers got their high adventure tales of action and spectacle, long before video games, comic books, or television. Every month, you could pick up a new issue of your favorite magazine for mere pennies and indulge in the excitement and creativity within its pages. It's hard to imagine now with the internet allowing constant connection to the outside world, but there was an entire industry built around delivering a continuous supply of entertainment to the reader, and that was the monthly pulp magazine.

So first it should be stated where they originated. In order to do that one must travel back far into a near-forgotten era of the relatively recent past.

Despite blowing up big during the early 20th century, the pulps actually have their roots from before then. One could mention fairy tales, penny dreadfuls, shared myths, and the like, where the tradition of startling and amazing stories sprang from. Instead, the focus should begin in a more modern frame with a man named Frank A. Munsey. He was the one who created the format for pulp magazines and ended up changing the landscape for tales of adventure forever. In many ways, he is responsible for just about every pop culture movement for decades to come.

On December 2nd, 1882, the first issue of *"Golden Argosy, Freighted with Treasures for Boys and Girls"* was released. It was thin at a mere eight pages, but still it remained the original, and very first, magazine he put out. Mr. Munsey already had much competition, as newspapers already had such stories in them, and dime novels existed at the time as well. Paper was not in short supply. The Industrial Revolution led to the process of creating cheap paper quickly. These advancements allowed for the production of larger magazines, so there were many other options for eager readers outside of mere magazines. Mr. Munsey was required to think outside the box if he wished to make a splash.

And that's what he did.

Altering the name of his magazine to *"Argosy"* in 1892, Mr. Munsey changed the format to an All-Fiction, all-ages format and used wood pulp for printing. At the time, new methods to create pulp paper were being forged, and he was paying attention to it. Automatic paper machines allowed for easy production of wood pulp paper, and they were getting more efficient all the time. By the time of the early 1900s, sulfite pulp had become the most common way to create wood pulp—but *Argosy* was already there at the forefront. Frank A. Munsey was ahead of his time. Paper production had never been easier. Just thirty years later the recovery boiler was invented which eventually allowed for the recycling of most production material in the pulping process, but by then *Argosy* was already the biggest pulp magazine in the world. Munsey was aware of all these changes, and was the first to take advantage of them. If anyone can be given credit for the success of pulp magazines, it should be him.

Munsey made this shift in production to pulp because he thought the stories more important than the quality of paper they were printed on. What mattered most to the audience, he figured, were the tales themselves. As long as they got them for a cheap price, the readers didn't care about anything else. Changing his mindset on paper production towards a story focus is what made the biggest difference for *Argosy*, and his gambit soon proved to be a genius move.

With this, he created the legendary *Argosy* magazine, which would go on to influence hundreds of other pulp magazines to come for decades to come. Stories of adventure and awe were sold for mere pennies every month. This is the first proper pulp magazine, and it remained the most popular throughout its over half-century run until the end of the pulps themselves. *Argosy* is still the magazine most synonymous with the pulps. Mr. Munsey achieved all this success by focusing on stories over the cost to the costumer. This was the attitude that became the core of the pulps.

Munsey's idea was a wonderful one in that by using wood pulp, the pulps, as they came to be called, saved on postage, could be sold for next to nothing by retailers, could be edited and compiled quickly, could easily be recycled, and were easy to stock up on for shops. Stories for the reader came first, and everyone else benefited. This approach was truly all about the adventures inside, and not for needlessly expensive packaging.

Beyond the packaging, there is also the content of the stories themselves.

There were no rules as to what Munsey could or could not run in his pages. Being that it was now for all ages instead of just children, he could run far more types of tales. He had no notion of genre and boundaries when running stories. One could have everything from romance to adventure to detective fiction to non-fiction and everything in between inside *Argosy's* pages, and no one would bat an eye. The readers would read anything, since it was aimed at every age and sex. It truly was an all-fiction format for an all-encompassing audience. Needless to say, others would jump on this bandwagon hoping to strike pay dirt, though it would take time for many to catch on as well as *Argosy* did. It isn't an exaggeration to say that Munsey changed everything, and his pulp magazines created an entire industry with aftershocks that are still being felt today.

To this day, *Argosy* remains the single most popular pulp magazine, and its influence is equal to none. If one wanted to understand the pulps, they could do worse than peruse one of its issues from back at the form's peak. The magazine truly was an innovator.

The market was beginning to shift, and it all centered on *Argosy* opening up the doors to all sorts of new stories. Companies such as Street & Smith followed not long after *Argosy's* success with their own attempts. It took a bit of time and experimentation, but, eventually, they struck gold.

Romance stories were their bread and butter, but they also put forth strides in the masked vigilante and hero genre with fare such as *The Shadow* and *Doc Savage*. If it could be imagined, then it probably had a magazine attached to it.

By 1923, the dime novel had all but vanished and was replaced with the much cheaper pulp format Munsey had already perfected. Now the form had become widespread and had become the standard. There was no place else to go for the inexpensive thrills the pulps offered.

Everyone wanted in, and everyone did get in. This made the stories included inside these magazines a total free-for-all. As hinted at above, genres didn't really exist in the pulps. The publishers did not shuffle their magazines around the sort of tropes modern readers are used to. In fact, their categorizations were a lot simpler and easier to understand. Just try to get a bead on the arguments of what people think Ray Bradbury should be categorized as these days, when back in the day his genre was the obvious weird tale. Back then, nobody really cared about such a thing.

Publishers were more interested in wowing and attracting the audience with adventure and awe than in showing off the paint job. Still, readers had their pick of the litter. There was no shortage of options during pulp's peak. If you could imagine it, you could read it.

By the middle of the Great Depression, there were over 200 pulp magazines in print. Despite suffering through true strife and misery, readers still wanted their good vs. evil wonder tales. It goes to show what the human soul truly desires when brought to its lowest: it's escapism. They faced grueling reality every day and didn't desire it in their fiction. Reading stories such as *A Princess of Mars* brought them joy and comfort.

Pulp readers were not any different than audiences are today. They all just want wonderment—to be brought higher. None of them, back in the day, were interested in tales of "realism" like the ones OldPub shovels out today.

For instance: the obsession with "realism" in fiction. Writers are told to write stories that must be "realistic" and somber in order to "relate" with readers. But despite the industry clinging to this belief, sales have not borne this out.

People who suffer real hardship want to be taken out of it: not revel in depravity. This is completely backwards from what modern writers are told when learning to become authors. "Realism" is not the answer.

Pulps were about pure imagination, and they sold like gangbusters. Take note how the titles of the magazines sold these pulps.

Common words and motifs used in magazine titles: *Adventure, Wonder, Amazing, Astounding, Detective, Dime, Western, Horror, Fight, Mystery, Love, Planet, Spicy, Strange, Super, Sport, Romantic, Terror, Thrilling, Uncanny,* and *Weird.* Phrases not used: Science Fiction and/or Fantasy. No obscure phrases or puns on popular movies or television shows. The titles outright tell you what you're getting inside. These magazines focused on pure excitement and paid little attention to aesthetics.

Pulps were sold primarily on inspiring awe before anything else. The romance of adventure and the terror of action were the selling points to those who wanted their precious escapism. You read pulps for excitement, for hope, for wonders, for horrors, and for love. You read them to be taken to higher and weirder places, away from your troubles. And people had plenty of troubles at the time.

Naturally, this meant they loved the pulps. Nothing offered escapism from their modern problems better than the pulps did.

So what is it that attracted the readers to these magazines, beyond their subject matter? What is it that tied their wild imagination and ideas together to make them so accessible?

That would be the heroes and villains inside their pages. There were plenty of them to go around, and audiences always love a good against evil story. Everyone can connect with heroes and villains. They exist in day to day life, after all.

Pulp heroes, often just average folks caught in weird situations, had to put up with intense threats and off-kilter plots that dragged them from their everyday, and normal, lives into madness and chaos. The leads of these adventures were just normal guys you'd find on the street, like your cousin Rick or Uncle Steve. The average pulp protagonist was an ordinary, healthy, and moral, person. You've met them before!

This was partially due to potential children and teenage readers and their needing role models to look up to. What better role models than those who strive to do the right thing? At the same time, there is something universal that pulls people together when a man strives to do his best despite evil facing him down. An adult can relate just as easily to this as younger readers, of course. And without the reliance on extreme explicit content, anyone could read these stories, and they did.

These dynamic, larger than life, and magnetic personalities are what drove readers to the pulps. Western heroes, like cowboys and sheriffs, naturally fit like a glove, as did the burgeoning detective story with their hard-boiled gumshoes. Many of these were normal people with a high skill level or specialized talent, perhaps even near-superhuman, and fought for the common man—for their country, and for civilization. Yes, these were white hats, used to unite the audience under one banner, where all readers could root for the same team. The pulp magazines were very pro-social, which made them welcoming to wary readers tired of the confusion of day to day life. This all-encompassing approach was one of the reasons these stories appealed to so many.

None of this means the pulps were shallow, as many insist today. A common refrain of the OldPub set is to declare a story with clear heroes and villains as trash: not murky, grey, or "realistic", enough for their refined tastes. This is backwards thinking.

Ironically, this thought process comes from not understanding what a white hat actually is. This type of protagonist hasn't actually been done correctly in mainstream entertainment for a long, long time now. OldPub, especially, cannot create a white hat protagonist to save their souls. This goes well with the fact that the current entertainment scene in the west could not be further away from the pulp spirit. They are essentially criticizing things completely out of their ability to create.

A white hat is just someone who knows what good is and fights for it. That is all. It doesn't mean that they don't stumble or that they don't fail to do the right thing at times but that they will always attempt to do what they know is right, sometimes without even realizing it themselves. The reason the pulp hero has endured for over a century is because he is immensely flexible outside of this setup. He's just a man, at the end of the day. He could be you or someone you know.

Nowhere is this flexibility more evident than the hard-boiled detective genre that emerged straight out the pulps. You want normal guys pushed to the limit? Then this genre is for you.

There were also mysterious heroes like The Shadow or Nick Carter who still fought to do the right thing despite incredible, and impossible, odds before them. They did this to keep the innocent safe, and to make the world a better place. It's something anyone can relate to, and audiences did.

What is important is that these building blocks of clear morality, dynamic protagonists, focus on action and adventure, and awe-inspiring locations, is what carried the pulp magazine into ruling what would become pop culture not that long later. This does not even factor in the cheap price, ease of availability, and vivid cover illustrations, to carry the load. Pulp magazines were the full package. This winning combination is why they had their success and why they lasted so long.

By the 1920s, the pulps were ruling the world. You could buy them just about anywhere and everyone read them. Their resulting influence would last to this very day. But they wouldn't stay at the top forever. Nothing does.

The descent of the pulp magazine took place in the 1940s, and the last holdouts died out in the 1950s. It should be clarified that the '20s and '30s are considered the peak of the pulp world by experts, and where the inspiration for the majority of the pop culture entertainment you still consume today comes from. It remains relevant even near a century removed from its creation. This would seem a very important thing to document in this modern world of pop culture obsession, but one rarely hears of it today.

By the 1950s, however, things were drying up for the magazines. New mediums began taking a piece of the pie, and the market splintered. World War II had caused production cost increases in pulp paper, and by the 1950s, they became too expensive to maintain. By the middle of the decade the old magazines were more or less gone, and the pulp story spun out into paperbacks, television, movies, and comic books. The magazines themselves could no longer be the force they once were.

Despite this, however, today their influence remains as strong as ever.

It is amazing how this simple, cheap form that lasted for over half a century, managing so much with so few limits, grew an influence that still exists to this day. But something was lost since their death. Those that sprang from the ruins of the pulps never had half the freedom they did back in the day, and the constricting nature of said later efforts is what led to so many follow-up industries' eventual death before the 20th century even closed. What remained of that pulp influence had all but been extinguished by the rise of OldPub and Hollywood. Nothing had quite the impact pulp fiction had when it began—it was a game changer, and few in those industries even realized it at the time. But that has changed, as you are now well aware. NewPub is that change.

Though it would be easy to talk down about cheap, common stories made for Joe Sixpack's beer money, the fact of the matter is they enjoyed a greater variety of fiction than the current OldPub audience does, and they were even sold for much better prices. You got far more bang for your buck back then, and there was something for just about everyone. It brought people together, and it lifted them higher while doing so.

Now, however, if you want pulp-inspired fiction, you have to scrounge around online and hope for the best or dig around used book stores for old yellowing pocket paperbacks. If you are reading this book you certainly understand how difficult it is to find classic pulp fiction today. The industry has done its best to bury its past.

The death of the pulps was a tragedy that the industry will never fully adapt to since that is where much of what their currently-fleeing audience enjoys originated from. As a result of this loss, OldPub is floundering and questioning where to go next, relying on out of touch editors and "experts" that are anything but for advice. Without those old silly stories of saucers, sorcerers, and silent assassins, they have little else left to offer potential audiences. They believe endlessly subverting adventure stories and heroism and being simultaneously "progressive" and nihilistic is the way to success.

But they're wrong. There is no future at the end of this blind alley. To go forward, they need to go back, retrace their steps, and work from there.

You now know why they don't do that, or have forgotten how to. Everything you read and enjoy, everything you grew up on, and everything that sparked your imagination as a child, has one foot in the pulps. Without accepting that, you can only to continue running from the past. Despite all this, OldPub has turned its back on pulp in exchange for smaller, more exclusive audiences that are not interested in real heroism or tales of astonishment. They no longer work for the money of the masses but for corporate approved cliques and elite circles. They don't want Joe Sixpack's beer money anymore.

So someone else has to do it instead. It is up to NewPub to pick up that slack and carry on this forgotten tradition the old industry has abandoned.

The long and short of it is that the pulps have an important piece in Western culture (and, eventually, worldwide among many different countries and places) for not only offering the biggest bang for the buck, but also letting anyone in who wanted to read and use his imagination. Pulps were for everyone, and everyone read them. They promoted the good and the true, and they lifted readers out of their doldrums while doing it. They did all of this for mere pennies, and all they asked was that you indulge in their weird worlds for a few hours of your time.

The pulp influence still exists, and it probably always will as long as the modern world does. Fast-paced adventures focused on excitement and astonishment will always have their place, and it will always be what audiences want deep in their hearts, even if they are taught to detest it by an industry that hates both the audience and the stories.

But how did this turnabout on the pulps come exactly? Did everyone wake up one day and realize the wonder stories they were reading were trash? Hardly. This will be tackled briefly later on, but for now there are a few major examples to mention. The smear job on the pulps was a concentrated effort from joyless critics and editors.

In October of 1937, a cadre of science fiction authors known as the Futurians produced a speech called "*Mutation or Death*" that was delivered at the Third Eastern Science Fiction Convention. This speech was written by writer John B. Michel and delivered by Donald A. Wollheim, future founder of DAW Books, and it has since garnered a reputation over the decades.

This speech proclaimed fantasy fiction's duty of being relevant and tackling social issues over entertaining the audience. Michel goes on about the importance of spreading propaganda to create a brighter future, and how it is the writer's duty to "mutate" the genre into something stronger than raygun and sorcerer stories. It is your duty to use your imagination to indoctrinate your audience.

Storytelling was no longer about pleasing the audience; it was about changing the audience. You are no longer working with them; they are now a block of clay to be shaped. This goes against the whole idea of art existing to connect the artist and the audience, and presents the massive ego at the heart of most anti-art movements. How can you connect with someone you look down on? You cannot.

While this speech was looked at as ridiculous at the time, the Futurians and those influenced by them did slip into editor positions and the like at the big publishers. They slowly nudged out the adventure fiction and replaced it with the social messaging fiction the genre has become today. They then started a campaign to tar the past and slander all those who came before them. The fact that even uttering the words "pulp fiction" (beyond the Tarantino movie) causes chuckles and sneers to most is proof of how successful this campaign was.

A perusal of the letter sections of later sword and planet magazines such as *Planet Stories* would show just how infectious this anti-pulp attitude became among "fandom" and the Futurian types. Adventure was taboo—you read to have propaganda dumped into your brain, and nothing else. Those that just wanted their weird tales could no longer get them.

Another issue was the rise of Scientism: the belief that science will solve all the world's ills. This philosophy was big in the early 20th century and much of the pulp era was spent both combating and indulging in it.

Editors such as John W. Campbell were more interested in science than adventure and turned *Astounding Stories*, one of the premier fantasy magazines into one focused on "fact" instead. The infamous *Weird Tales* had countless stories about the need for more in life than just what one could see before his eyes, even if it did delve into some bizarre spiritualist themes. Campbell even created *Unknown Magazine* in order to combat fantasy itself and give the supernatural a scientific explanation.

In other words, fantasy no longer became about what you could do—it became about what you couldn't do. And these are the ones who seized control of the industry during the days of the pulps. The last thing the fanatics wanted were readers who could freely use their imagination.

All of this came together to form an industry that was deliberately anti-pulp, and it has remained as such for decades, getting creakier and rustier with each passing generation. And now the whole castle is collapsing.

It has been over half a century removed from the end of the pulps, and people are still talking about them and creating in their image. This book's existence alone is proof of that. They've never died, despite so many attempts to do them in that continue to this day from character assassination to deliberate lack of reprinting. The ideas they propagated and the techniques they taught writers still exist, and their influence remains stronger than ever. This is where the industry came from, and where it needs to return to.

Again, the pulp mindset is about understanding a rich past and pulling it forward into the present in order to create for the future. Art is about reconnecting to the past in order to address the future. This is what OldPub has lost, and what you must gain.

Now that you understand what pulp is and where it came from it is time to move from the past to the present. How can this pulp mindset be applied today, and can it truly still appeal as it once did?

Of course it can. Tales of adventure never will go out of date, and neither will heroism. It might not be 1896 anymore, but the same rules from back then still apply today. Write for the audience and give them what they want.

There are new pulp authors born every day, and you can be one of them. In the next chapter, you will learn just how. All it takes is the right mindset.

The Pulp Mindset

In the new publishing world, being a pulp writer is just about the only way to survive. You more or less are required to be one to put out enough material in order to keep your audience's attention. Magazines might be long gone, but the approach to production remains the same. The audience wants constant content, and only those with a pulp mindset can provide it for them.

In these crazy days of modern publishing, it doesn't feel like there's any real formula for success. That's because there isn't. It used to be that getting your name on the cover of a magazine was the way to get your foot in the door. Then, it was writing short stories that would catch the attention of a publisher who would ask for a novel. After that period in publishing, it was about getting an agent who would deal with traditional publishing companies on your behalf, and then you would get your book on the shelves of the big chains stores where everybody could see it. You might not have been the next Dean Koontz, but at least you traced his steps, and that was good enough. Perhaps you would eventually get that hit to break out of the midlist—as long as you listened to the very hip and with it editors, that is. At least, that's how the experience was sold.

Reality was much different. Getting a hit wasn't as simple as just checking the right boxes on some magical "good storytelling" list. At the same time, independent publishers were scooped up by the big dogs throughout the 1970s and '80s; the rules were becoming more and more consolidated. Imagination was ceding ground to these makeshift formulas created by higher-ups with questionable motives and dubious results.

However, during this not-too-subtle sea change from writing for pulp magazines into scribing out phonebook-sized tomes in the 20th century, much was lost sight of along the way. The industry went from stories between 1,000 to 40,000 words in length, into stories needing to be over

80,000 words just to be considered publishable by OldPub. Naturally, this move vastly changed the landscape of the industry by limiting the variety of stories one could write.

This was a shift that happened back in the age of *Argosy* at the start of the 20th century to the days of *"The Wheel of Time"* by the end. These two styles couldn't be more different from each other, and yet they both spun out of the same industry in less than one hundred year period. It goes without saying that something would need to have changed along the way for this to occur and not be noted as odd by those paying attention. While longer books always existed, they were not as long as fantastical books would come to be by the close of the 20th century. H. Rider Haggard and Robert Louis Stevenson could never imagine writing an adventure the size of *"The Stand"* by Stephen King or a series as long and padded as *The Wheel of Time* was. A shift had occurred.

Nothing changes a full 180 degrees from what it once was without losing a significant chunk of its identity in the process. That's just not possible. The entire market mutated by an almost comical degree over this relatively short period of time.

Of course, none of this is to say *Wheel of Time* is a bad series or that the pulp format was the better way to go, but to say there is nothing of value worth keeping from the pulp era, as acolytes of OldPub insist to this day, is patently absurd. It is absurd because the audience during the pulp era was far larger and broader than what it was by century's end, as was its content.

Times have also changed since the 1990s. *The Wheel of Time* approach is no longer feasible for authors and was never right for a segment of customers who wanted something else but weren't being offered it. OldPub's ways are dated, and yet they are still set in them.

The uncomfortable truth for the industry is that the 1990s are over, and the overstuffed book in an endless series parsed out over an interminable period of time is not a way to make a living as a writer anymore. It isn't what audiences go for. What you learn from modern writing courses and How-To books today is from a crop who still teaches outdated information to aspiring writers that are blissfully unaware at how different the field is now. There is an entire industry that is centered on telling aspiring authors what they want to hear instead of what they need to understand. You are no longer limited by borders put up by the old system, and you don't need anyone telling you what to do.

This might seem like a strange thing to say in a guide on pulp writing, but, as you already know, this isn't a How-To book meant to give you secret tips to be a million selling author. It's a book about understanding the state of things as they are and how to adapt to these changes. In these modern times, there are a few truths that must be faced if one wishes to be a writer, but few wannabe authors are ever told what they are.

For one thing, less people in the modern world than ever before actually read. No one is going out of their way to buy the newest OldPub book, and the last remaining big book chain is sliding towards compete irrelevancy and bankruptcy in this age of online shopping. The audience is not getting what they want from this mess of an industry, and they are walking away.

But they once did get what they wanted, and they can get it again. All it takes is the right mindset.

In the era of the internet, social media, tablets, and smartphones, the audience that exists wants quick and punchy entertainment. People today watch online videos far more than they watch television. Streaming services get more attention than traditional cinemas do. Entire music hosting sites and subcultures have supplanted Record and CD stores. The 21st century is an entire different world than the one it was even a decade ago.

The writing industry, meanwhile, has remained entrenched in outdated ideas taught by shambling dinosaurs. They teach with an anti-pulp and anti-traditionalist mindset as if their world is still New York City in the 1970s. Readers are being left in the dust while other mediums adapt to a changing landscape. This happened because OldPub has paid no attention to the shifting culture. One glance at the price of their ebooks should show as such.

Of course, it is obvious they keep their ebook prices high to keep their bookstore chains in business, but that is merely delaying the inevitable. They are running on borrowed time. Perhaps dinosaur industry isn't strong enough—would amoebic be a better descriptor of their irrelevance?

The issue is that this traditional pulp mindset they abandoned is what the writing industry needs in order to survive this culture shift. Unlike the other entertainment industries, writing should be the easiest to adapt to this new landscape, but OldPub has utterly failed to do so. To get with the times, writers need to throw away the subversive thinking and habits that got the industry to the situation where it is today. It needs to hit the reset button.

First, it should be mentioned what damaged these old ways and who it was that replaced them with the stale scene the industry is now. To understand why one must go back to their roots they should see who it was that dug them up to begin with.

As mentioned earlier, the Futurians and editors such as John W. Campbell aided in this change, but there were others who came on after to continue swinging the wrecking ball.

For instance, there were critics in the world of fantastical writing that did tremendous damage to the fantastical itself; their opinions seeping into literature courses still taught today as if gospel truth. And no, these experts weren't even bestselling authors. Nonetheless, their rules reign supreme.

One critic in particular who did much damage was one with the imagination of a grape-nut, and yet still ended up being the final word on the fantastical. How he got to that position is anyone's guess. This self-proclaimed master was a critic and writer named Damon Knight.

Damon Knight was a bit of a firebrand in his day. People thought him subversive and insightful as he tore down and ruined the careers of such writers as A.E. Van Vogt, who had helped usher in a Silver Age in his field, and Mr. Knight ripped him apart with manic glee. Knight also crafted the narrative that Robert. E. Howard, creator of Conan the Barbarian and Solomon Kane, and therefore one of the most important writers of the 20th century, was a deviant freak who had a mother obsession which is why he committed suicide at a young age. Knight was not a very tactful man, and some of his criticisms were outright absurd.

Damon Knight is most famous for his ironically named *"Book of Wonder,"* which contains his usual brand of vitriol dipped in thirty cent words, and a glorious misunderstanding of what wonder actually is. But that subject will come later. For now, it is important to note that he was no friend of the pulps, nor of imagination. The irony is that the man who self-admitted to not understanding the appeal of H.P. Lovecraft or Robert E. Howard is the one who is going to tell you what wonder is and will have tremendous influence in the industry the former two helped define. Someone who hates his roots is not one who can explain their appeal, yet this is what happened.

Beyond critics, there are writer's workshops such as Clarion. Now, Clarion itself was not quite as hateful as Mr. Knight, but it also didn't help new writers much. In fact, the entire industry of writer's workshops catering to those who desire the image of tortured artist more than being a writer ended up damaging their focus. Writer's workshops simply are not necessary to be a writer, but the only people who don't know this are aspiring writers. It is quite the mystery as to how it all ended up this way.

You do not need a writer's course to become a writer. You do not need formulas beat into your brain, by people who don't sell as much as the grand-masters, telling you how to be more successful than them. All you need to do is learn to do it by yourself. The biggest sin of writer's workshops is charging people to learn things they could learn on their own with practice or through a good editor. It isn't like skills involving power tools or moving mechanical parts—all you need to be a writer is to read and to absorb.

However, the worst damage Clarion itself did to the industry was a movement created over fifteen years ago, as of this writing. That would be the Mundane Science Fiction Movement.

The Mundane Movement was about making sure impossible things stay out of impossible fiction. No warp drives, magic, ghosts, or aliens. It was a way of being "realistic" about forward-looking fiction and making sure writers rein it in. This way you can project a "realistic" future that can better teach the audience social issues and not get distracted by that pesky escapism. No one apparently told them that this approach is the antithesis of both awe and the point of the genre in question.

Audiences do not go to art for "realism": they go to art to be entertained and to be excited. This anti-wonder movement is the sort of thinking that has chased so many readers away from OldPub. After graduating high school, most teenagers never pick up a book ever again, and it is due to them being taught this sort of anti-art rhetoric and being told this is the way literature should be. This is what reading is, and if you don't like it you can leave. Guess what these potential readers choose to do?

Thankfully, those ways are on the way out. To be a pulp writer, you must throw that outdated thinking away.

If you want to be a pulp writer, you want to reach the widest possible audience for your story. The field has already contracted to a comically small degree due to OldPub's shenanigans such as the ones mentioned above. They do not know how to reach a wider audience, because they do not wish to. They are more interested in being high priests of literature and teaching readers the correct things to think. Therefore, if you want to get a reader base there is no point listening to them. OldPub has long since forgotten they were selling art, not propaganda.

The only example from the recent past we can use to follow into the future is those of the old masters, long since erased by acolytes of the modern industry. They were the last to truly be successful in giving the audience what they wanted.

Not to beat a dead horse, but the pulp magazines allowed more freedom for writers in its strict audience-first formula than what later became the standard in OldPub. In an age where audiences want more content in shorter bursts of time, releasing a single 100,000 word tome every half-decade is simply no longer sustainable or desired. The audience will not wait for it, and the writer could be busy writing more stories that would sell just as well (or better) in the interim. The age of fat, barely edited, doorstoppers is over. The fast-paced information age demands a similarly condensed and sharp story that offers everything those books could offer, only in less space. No one did this better than the pulps did, and that makes them the best mentor for the NewPub writer.

To be a pulp writer in this ever-changing space, you have to do as they did. This means writing every single day and putting out content for readers on a constant basis. It also means making sure your stories are exciting and full of movement and that you deliver a satisfying end. These stories must also do all of this in the least amount of words you can manage.

This will be explained in more detail in the chapters to come, but for now, it is enough to say that this is the complete opposite of the OldPub approach. It isn't about the artist's ego—it's about delivering product to costumers. What is important is to gain a mindset that they don't teach in those pricey classes in the urban metropolises.

A reader just wants to be entertained, and a writer's job is to entertain them. The success of the original pulps proves this. Some will be more entertained than others no matter what you do, as is always the case, but a pulp writer needs to make sure their story appeals to the largest amount of people interested in said style of story. A writer shouldn't strive for cult appeal; that isn't a reliable or easy status to obtain. Few writers make money in OldPub, even when working a second job, and they actually *are* aiming for cult appeal. You need to aim higher and shoot farther than they do.

Do you write action? Then you need to include the best action you can. Do you write mystery? Then you need to include the most labyrinthine twists you can think of. Do you write horror? Then you need to thrill your audience with the most grotesque ideas hiding in the shadows of your wildest dreams. Always aim high and cast the net wide by sharpening your focus. Always offer the purest possible experience in your genre of choice. Believe it or not, normal people like your sort of stories, too. They're just waiting for someone to actually write for them again.

Pulp writers back in the day aimed wide by not deliberately alienating audiences or telling their readers what they "really" wanted. All readers want are stories that hit them dead on with the force of a hurricane. Straightforwardness—being clear and not clever—is what they desire. So few in OldPub even think to offer that these days.

It should be noted that desiring simplicity doesn't mean readers are simpletons and should be talked down to or given substandard product. It just means the writer should be talking *to* them—not over or through them instead. This is art—your job is to *connect* to your audience. You cannot connect with someone if you feel you are above them.

The rules are actually very simple. In fact, there's only really one big law no writer should ignore: Don't violate the reader's trust.

You can deliver plot twists to your audience; you cannot promise them an action story and then deliver a non-fiction account of dolphin riding in Florida. Give them what they came for. Subversion is not a synonym for "good" and it is about time that becomes common knowledge once more.

Know when to let the hero and the princess ride off into the sunset together. The audience is coming to you for entertainment; they aren't coming for you to tell them the hero is a villain and the princess is actually a figment of his broken brain. Can you write a story with that as a twist? Yes, as long you don't violate the reader's innate sense that heroism is real, that good exists, and that everything up to that twist hasn't been a waste of their time. They all share this deeper understanding on what stories need, and you should avoid toying with that inherent knowledge at your own risk.

Unfortunately, many modern writers (especially in OldPub) cannot help showing how brilliant their twists are, which leaves their potentially-exciting stories limp and flat with nothing to them but said shallow table flip. A story is a journey—a twist along the way is not the point of a journey. Know what the majority of your audience is looking for and write to that instead. Do not risk trying to fool your readers by deceiving them with flashy twists that undercut the beginning of the story. It will not end well for you.

You are not writing for a deliberately small fraction of a fraction of your genre that enjoys meaningless twists: as stated before, an artist's job is to connect with people through their art. It is not to tell your audience how to think or believe—they are smart enough to be reading your books, which means they are smart enough to think for themselves. A writer's job is to present their story as clearly as possible to the reader. You aren't there to challenge your audience; you are there to journey with them.

The artist is on the patron's side; he is not their opponent.

This is the key to writing pulp in the modern world. Write fast, connect with readers, and let your imagination run wild. Don't hinder yourself with boundaries the greats never had. In this hi-speed age, you need every advantage and tool you can get. That means going back to basics to when the two sides were on the same page. The NewPub age is about reclaiming what was forgotten by the dying dinosaur industry that readers are leaving behind.

By being a pulp writer, you will have an advantage few others will, including those paying thousands of dollars for writing classes do not. You have a better and stronger tradition on your side, and it is one with a proven track record of success. That is success in the form of audience satisfaction. Sales are never guaranteed in the world of art, but audience satisfaction is something you can learn to achieve.

Becoming a pulp writer doesn't mean you will gain a sure-fire formula for writing best-selling stories. It doesn't guarantee selling hundreds of thousands of books—but it guarantees you more opportunities of getting to that point. The more productive you are, the more chances you have of getting that hit that will put you over the top. The only way to win at the game is to play.

The pulp mindset is a way of thinking that prioritizes writing, the customer, and imagination, over all else. This is about stripping entertainment down to bare essentials in an age where it appears those factors have been forgotten for artist ego. They are what the profession used to be about, and will be about again.

With this mindset you can conquer anything. To be a pulp writer one must have the tools, the drive, and the right thought process. The future is pulp, and it is time to get used to it.

But you might be asking what to write and how to write it? How exactly does one write a pulp tale? Can it really be as simple as just writing an action story?

Should you find yourself asking these questions then you are ready to move on to the next stage. In the following chapter, we will focus on these very questions.

How to Write Pulp

Previous chapters have established that the pulp mindset is about developing a way of working and thinking that will alter the way you approach fiction writing. You now understand how invaluable it is to being a new creative in today's landscape.

That said, there are those who would read this book and still have no idea where to even begin when starting to write, never mind in a maligned area such as pulp writing. Some tips and tricks need explaining, especially considering the only other option for some starting writers is to sign up for overpriced writing seminars. Since this is a book about gaining a pulp mindset, some practical advice is required, though it should be stressed again that this is not the overall point of this guide.

Nonetheless, this is an elephant in the room that needs addressing. Should you desire to learn in-depth ways to write there are more expansive books, blogs, and online videos, on the subject available—this chapter will focus only on simple basics to get you started.

How does one actually write pulp? Is it just the same writing style as OldPub only with more explosions and WWI biplanes? Is it merely an aesthetic? Is it mindless fluff?

No, that is just a shallow interpretation of pulp writing. The issue is that there is no one out there to tell upcoming writers the truth. There is no "How to Write Pulp" writer's workshop one can waste hundreds of dollars on in order to learn this. Most authors simply assume writing "pulp" is the tacky aping of 1920s décor, clothing, and lingo, and little else. Unfortunately, that misses the entire point of how pulp stories gained their popularity back in the day. It wasn't as simple as a specific image.

The biggest stumbling block with becoming a writer is learning exactly how you are supposed to write. There are many writing courses, lectures, and pieces of advice you can get out in the wild, but most are contradictory, outdated, or just plain incorrect. Some are actively harmful. Sorting through that is a hard enough task for an upstart author, especially now with the internet offering so much information overload. At the same time, most of what is out there is completely antithetical to becoming a pulp writer.

Don't expect that much in the way of practical advice in this chapter. The fact of the matter is that no writer really knows what makes their work popular. Their own writing advice books would be producing million sellers by the bucket load were that the case, which clearly has not happened. There is no formula for guaranteed success, not even from those who have experienced it.

However, there is a correct mindset and right attitude to have that will allow you to acquire the basic skills and work ethic to reach your goal of becoming a writer. Writing is a craft, and, like every other craft, it needs to be practiced many times over a long period before it is good enough to present to the public. Even professional writers do not sell their first drafts. Writing sellable prose takes effort, but there are some things you can do in the meantime to help get moving in the right direction. Being a pulp writer is not very complex, it just requires narrow focus.

The first step is to read old pulp works from before the 1940s when they were at peak popularity. See what worked, and learn what they have to teach. These works are easier to find than ever before. Many are now in the public domain and can be found for free in online libraries such as archive.org or Project Gutenberg. Amazon even sells packs of short stories written by the masters for as low as a dollar. Put in a search for what interests you. There is plenty out there to sift through, but if you want to write with a pulp mindset you should familiarize yourself with how the master pulp writers worked and what they put out. Writers should read.

As for specific examples, it would depend on what your chosen genre is and where you want to direct your energy. Read heavily in that area before moving on to others. Sharpening up the basics should come before turning a focus to more advanced works.

The biggest and most influential writers during the peak of the pulp era were as follows:

- Lord Dunsany
- Edgar Rice Burroughs

- Abraham Merritt
- Frederick Faust (Writing as "Max Brand")
- H.P. Lovecraft
- Robert E. Howard
- Walter B. Gibson (writing as "Maxwell Grant")
- Lester Dent (writing as "Kenneth Robeson")
- Raymond Chandler
- Dashiell Hammett
- E.E. "Doc" Smith
- Sax Rohmer
- Zane Grey
- Carroll John Daly

Now, there are hundreds of other writers worthy of inclusion, some of which are on the level with the above, but these authors are the ones who created and heavily influenced what it is you grew up on and still enjoy to this day. At this time, take note of these writers and burn them into your brain. You are not going to want to forget them.

For further examples of great pulp writers, you can look up the magazines *Weird Tales*, *Black Mask*, *Adventure*, *Planet Stories*, *Blue Book*, *Short Stories*, and *Argosy*, and pour through their pages. There are dozens of writers worth discovering in those magazines, many of which are still influential and beloved today. You have no shortage of worlds to discover.

These pulp authors all more or less started everything currently being milked dry and subverted in modern pop culture. If you want to write in these genres, you really should read these old writers. There are many ideas here that have been subverted and tremendously diluted by modern day Hollywood and OldPub.

Of course, those in charge of these Proterozoic industries have tried their best to bury, deconstruct, and bend, these writers to their own end, so you will have to go in with a sharper mind than they have taught you to. Take note of how these authors put together a tale, and apply it to your own work. Art is a tradition: it is meant to be passed down. You are carrying on a legacy, so treat it seriously.

After this, move on to other writers in the same era. You will find no shortage of excellent examples of creators constructing a sharp pulp tale. In fact, you have over half a century of writers to work through! You will never have to bother with a lazy Hollywood adaptation of these works ever again. Happy reading!

Next, you must learn how exactly to take those ideas from your head and put them to paper. This is the trickiest place to begin without some sort of guide. This is what leads so many aspiring artists to buy dozens of How-To-Write books that are all stuffed with vastly different pieces of advice. This isn't that strange. Writers, like all artists, have many different styles and ways to put their wildest thoughts to paper. Naturally, this means their advice will vary tremendously.

Pulling those words from your head and putting them down on paper in a coherent way is the primary job of a writer. This stands to reason that prose is your first stumbling block to becoming one. This is where it is time to go into a bit of practical advice.

Common knowledge is that you need to write over one million words of junk before your prose even approaches being sellable. There is truth to this. Writing is a craft, and it must be developed just as woodworking or car repair; however, there are tips to help you get on the right track sooner than you might think.

Try the following tricks to help knock your prose writing into shape.

First, do not start with writing novels. This is where every fledgling modern writer tries their hand, and it is always a bad place to begin. Think about it: mountain climbers do not scale Mount Everest on their first climb. Neither should new writers begin with the longest form of story. And yet, they always do.

You have been trained by OldPub to think that the fat thousand page paperback is the only sort of story that matters and the one the audience is dying for. A new writer starting out is going to think this is their path to success and will begin writing over 100,000 words of aimless junk without even getting to an ending because this is what they think they have to do. They might even throw their hands up and declare writing isn't for them before finishing a single draft. It kills drive and motivation much too early.

Should you follow the above advice to read the pulp masters, however, you will learn that there are other ways to write stories. For one, pulp tales could be any length. They could be anything from short stories to novelettes to novellas and, yes, novels. Most of these works do not exceed 60,000 words, unlike the bloated works in OldPub. This is the groove where you want to concentrate your writing. Start smaller and in a more sharp form than the overstuffed and sluggish modern OldPub novel.

This will also help to produce works in a form the public actually demands. The modern market wants quantity in number more than in girth. Putting out three 30,000 word books instead of one 90,000 word book triples your chances of someone finding you and buying your novels. The more books you release, the more you increase your chances of success. This is one of NewPub's biggest advantages over the sluggish release schedules of OldPub. Authors can do more with less space.

This is why new writers should start with short stories first. They need to learn craft on a smaller scale without getting overwhelmed with secondary issues like heavy world building or subplots or a bloated and unwieldy cast. This smaller focus has an additional effect in training the new writer to sharpen their prose and their storytelling and learn to better use the space afforded them. Start small and work your way up.

How about writing schedules? Are you still having trouble with finding the time to write? Not everyone has hundreds of free hours to dedicate to writing, after all. If you are struggling, here are some tips to use in order to learn basic writing in a more manageable fashion.

Should the new writer write at least 500 words a day, which is very doable, he could be finished a short story in a week. That is much faster than starting on a phone book-sized novel that the novice writers stumbles through over the course of (at least) a year. This will allow them to learn things such as pacing, build up, and endings, in a much easier fashion.

Simply outline the points in the story you want to hit and then write it out accordingly. You will be done in a jiffy and ready for the next project.

The author of *Doc Savage*, Lester Dent himself, had a formula for pulp writing. In summation, you need a new event to occur every block of 2,500 words, each moment escalating from the last. This amount can be scaled depending on the form of the story from flash fiction all the way up to a novel. The author simply needs to pace it out accordingly. What you want to do is keep the audience hooked while heightening the stakes with each passing moment, even if subtly.

But this doesn't quite help with improving the prose itself, does it? The most frightening part for a new writer is merely typing the words themselves and questioning if they are doing it correctly. The entire process feels daunting, like treading water in the deep end after your first swimming lesson. After all, you see swaths of aspiring writers on social media go on about how tough it is to just put words on the page. That makes it sound like writing is a frightening and torturous prospect.

It's not. These aspiring writers simply think too much of themselves and aren't willing to get down in the dirt and do the work. Learning to write takes a long time, but it isn't a complicated process.

There are easy tricks one can use to learn in order to structure a basic sentence. Enough practice and you will have it burned into your brain.

The best way to improve prose quickly is to find two books whose prose you want to write like, then pick two paragraphs from each that strikes your fancy. Next, write the paragraphs out double-spaced by hand on a piece of paper. It might take some time, but it will stick in your head better if it is done via pen or pencil.

Lastly, note in the margins above each word where the nouns, pronouns, verbs, adjectives, and adverbs, lay. Do this enough and basic sentence organization will become clearer. It also gives you an idea of flow and pacing on the sentence level.

Do this for at least a month, in addition to your normal 500 words, and you will hardly believe how much you've learned in such a short time. Keep it up until basic sentence construction is second nature to you.

Once again, here are the steps for a daily schedule of writing:

1) Write out a paragraph double-spaced
2) Note in the lines above where all the nouns etc. are located
3) Repeat three more times
4) Write out 500 words of your short story

Practice is the best way to learn a craft, and this sort of practice will allow a new writer to learn faster.

Now, while the above might help with the prose, there is another aspect of writing to consider beyond that. This would be the bane of many older readers and the stumbling block of many newer writers: the dialogue.

Dialogue writing is a whole other skill to learn outside basic prose construction. It's not as simple as writing out long-winding conversations and letting the characters do the heavy lifting for your storytelling. The last thing your dialogue should do is tell the audience what the prose should already be showing them. Dialogue exists to either advance a story or reveal an important character trait that has plot relevance. It should not be used to reveal bits of information irrelevant to either. Writers shouldn't waste their readers' time.

Another issue about dialogue is that in this more visual age, most have grown up with movies and television as their primary inspiration. This means newer writers get their notion of how speech should sound from said mediums instead of from books.

However, book dialogue is entirely different from what you see on the screen. As you now know, pulp writing needs to be brisk and powerful. Your dialogue should be no different. It should be straightforward and revealing, but not irrelevant or convoluted. It has to matter as much as the prose does.

Unfortunately, too many writers today are inspired by *Buffy the Vampire Slayer's* Joss Whedon. They mimic his quip-filled snarky dialogue and think every bit of their own dialogue needs to be peppered with jokes or pop culture references like his was. This is not the way to write pulp, and is quite obnoxious to most readers.

An example of such dialogue:

> The phone rang her familiar *Happy Days* ringtone, and she couldn't help but let it play out before picking it up. That song always lightened her day. Luckily, the caller was her best friend Becky. Susan had been waiting all day for this call.
>
> "Hey," Susan said.
>
> Becky giggled. "What's up?"
>
> "My stress levels after my boss caught me texting during the meeting. Dude is so serious it's like the anti-Heath Ledger. Why so serious, right?"
>
> "Yikes!"
>
> "Very yikes. Cringier than the climax of *Xanadu*, only without the catchy music! I bet he listens to nu metal like it's 1999. He's such a total uptight relic. Yuck. I could use a break."
>
> "Well, you're in luck. I've got a lead on your brother's killer."

There's a lot of nonsense in that passage that makes it bad, but there are two obvious reasons it simply does not work. The first problem is that every bit of that lousy scene could be edited down to one exchange. It's wasting the reader's time with irrelevant nonsense.

The second issue is that it absolutely kills any sort of serious tone when characters are not treating the stakes properly. She's looking for her brother's killer: why is she acting like a valley girl teenager from the 1980s? This tone will take any normal reader out of the situation and it devalues any threat in the plot. It is also obnoxious to read, and it's distracting.

Tone, build up, and atmosphere, are three important aspects of writing important to pulp. All three require a tight leash. In a style that relies on action to thrive, these are the most invaluable tools a writer can use in the space they have.

Here is the above exchange edited down:

> After a long day, she slumped in her easy chair and sighed. The boss could be such a drag. Suddenly, the phone rang. She hardly noticed until the ringtone had almost completed its full ridiculous length. It was the call she had been waiting for—her friend Becky was finally getting back to her.
>
> "There you are!" Susan said, half-yawning. "Any news?"
>
> "It was hard searching, but I think I found the lead on your brother's killer."

That's it. You could add a line or two, or perhaps make it even shorter, but that is the gist of what you need. The nonsense has been gutted, and the intent is clear.

That is what writing is: being clear enough to not let your writing get in the way of the story.

All of the above should be more than enough to get you on the right track. With enough practice you will internalize what works and will be able to add it to your own developing toolkit. Up next comes the real trick of the trade: applying it to your own stories!

The first step of being pulp is cranking out the words, and with these simple steps anyone will be well on their way to churning out the right ones they need for their story. That is half the battle.

But while the words might be the right ones does that mean the story itself will be pulp? Not necessarily. Aside from the craft, there is also the authorial intent. Pulp is action-based storytelling.

In order to understand the pulp mindset beyond the words being placed on the page, one needs to take two separate, but equally important, factors into consideration when constructing a story—that would be action and wonder. The content itself matters just as much as these do. However, that is getting ahead of the purpose of this particular chapter.

For now, it is enough to just write and get the words in the right shape needed. This should be the first priority for a new writer. Practice over and over as many times as it takes to get the prose you desire. Once that is accomplished, next comes what you do with those words you worked so hard to create. What sort of story should a pulp tale be?

As stated earlier, what you do with these new tools you have just acquired is create stories of action and wonder. Now to learn just how to do that.

Get to the Action!

Chances are that if you are reading this book, you wish to make a living off your art. You don't just want to be a pulp writer: you want to be successful. If that is the case then you must invest in learning to write action.

One of the most well-known clichés of the pulps is that they are solely about mindless violence, sex, and vague politically-incorrect behavior. While this might be true of some of what released back then, it is horribly reductionist and not representative of the best the pulps had to offer. Low art relies on visceral emotion to connect with customers, so this is what the authors relied on.

However, there is one thing about which that above cliché is correct. Pulp stories are primarily about action, and being a pulp writer means being an action writer. There is simply no way to avoid this truth. This is the one thing no modern writing class will ever teach you—writing action is an invaluable skill, especially in the creation of low art.

At this point, you might be questioning just what this "low art" is. If there is a low art, then what is high art? Can't you create one as easily as the other? Is this just a term created to make bad artists feel better about themselves? The answers to these questions might surprise you.

Bringing up the "What is art?" question tweaks a lot of noses, when the elephant in the room is that every product created is art. It's just a matter of how good said art is. However, there are different types of art that every creator should be aware of. This would be the reason why they are separated into categories such as low art and high art.

First of all, there is a difference between the two, and secondly, no, they are not interchangeable. The two require entirely different skill sets to create. Low art deals with visceral and tangible goals and stakes, while high art deals with ephemeral and heady concepts. They are two sides of the same coin, and one who writes one will not adapt so easily to the other. If you wish to be a pulp writer, then you must master the craft of low art creation.

If you're reading a book by Dostoevsky or Flannery O'Connor, you are not there to be greeted with fast-paced stories of heroes shooting villains and rescuing space princesses. This sort of fiction exists for an entirely different reason than the pulps. People pick up an adventure book for the thrill of it all, not to examine their souls and learn more about why we are here and where we are going. High art is made to dwell in more complex spaces, while low art deals in excitement. You read high art to understand higher things, not to be pulled into a globe-trotting yarn.

What low art exists for is this escapism, and it does this with its greatest weapon: action.

It should first be pointed out that the meaning of "action" in this context is not simply referring to violence or fight scenes. There is more to action than fist-fights and car explosions, though those are certainly welcome! That is merely one piece of the pie. Even infamously over-the-top action movies from the 1980s aren't constant gunfights. They allow scenes to breathe and be set-up before it gets to those thrilling sequences. It is still storytelling, after all. The audience still wants a plot.

"Action" means "movement": the story needs to keep flowing. From sentence to sentence and word to word, the audience wants to be taken to a new world and wants to stay there. This is what "action" is about in a pulp context: it is about keeping the reader there in that new world. To do this the tale has to always be moving, not pondering or plodding along.

A pulp story blitzes from point to point in as few words as possible, culminating in a conclusion that neatly wraps up everything before with a bow. It is a rollercoaster of excitement where every part is necessary to keep the ride moving and the car on the tracks. This is an entirely different craft than high art, and it's one many self-important artists could stand to learn.

This is action-based writing, and your storytelling should reflect that pacing. This is your bread and butter.

Ultimately, pulp writing is now exclusively the property of NewPub. This happened due to neglect on OldPub's part, which chased away potential readers who wanted low art and couldn't get it. You will find no action-first storytelling coming out of the dinosaur industry that isn't a reprint, outside of the standard thriller genre. OldPub has no advice when it comes to action writing, because they have forgotten that action means. They are out of touch with what the audience wants.

This means you cannot rely on a few outdated tropes that have crept into adventure fiction over the decades due to the influence of OldPub, lingering like stink on cheese. Writing workshops and instructors still insist on spreading advice that hampers action storytelling. New writers are not going to realize there is a problem due to their blind trust of these institutions. This mess is what has created the need for books such as the one before you to exist.

Here are a few tips and tricks for writers to get to the action as soon as they can.

To start with, be sure to begin your story focused on the main character. The tale's very first sentence needs to be an immediate hook that drags the reader kicking and screaming into the protagonist's world. To do this, the audience do not need to see the scenery or know about the local wildlife: they need to understand who they are following, and why. Bam! Here's your protagonist, and here is why he matters! The sooner this is done the sooner the reader is invested.

The story needs to start here because you need your reader to care about your character as soon as possible. You need to set up stakes at the closest, most opportune time. The reader needs to open the book and instantly be grabbed by the throat.

This is pulp writing—hit 'em where it hurts!

Example

"Sonny Brunch woke up with a splitting headache, which went well with the decapitated body lying next to him in the brick alley."

Character introduced, setting established, and interest piqued. You did this in the very first sentence, and you didn't have to rely on any sort of hacky literary trick taught in today's workshops. That is pulp: get in and get out. You have the reader hooked in, and now you can carry them through on the edge of their seat.

The old cliché about the pulps was that they were rollercoasters. There is a lot of truth to this in that the story does need to keep moving. But that also means you have to know when to pull your punches to create tension and intrigue, just as a rollercoaster slows down at inclines.

There are tips to keep their eyes to the page even at a break in the action. You will need to write your chapters as if you were writing a serial in a pulp magazine. Every chapter needs to end on a hook, a reveal, or an important question that will lead the reader directly into the next one. It has to give the audience less opportunity to put your book down and give them more reasons to come back. You do not want to let them off the ride for even a second.

Those cheesy serials you heard mocked so much actually did have some good ideas. One of them is that they knew how to keep audiences coming back for more. Does modern Hollywood understand this? Not so much. So which of the above two should you look to for advice?

Since every chapter should end with a hook, it stands to reason every chapter has to begin with the ball already rolling. After an initial setup to remind the reader just what the protagonist is doing, the action continues straight away. This brisk pace carries throughout the story, keeping the reader in their seats just that one second longer until they just realized they stayed up until 3am to finish the book. It's your job to make sure to keep the story rolling until the brakes finally creak at the last station. This approach leaves no room for fat or flab—pure movement is a requirement.

So yes, pulp writing is about action. The old magazines were cheap, disposable, and trashy. But that doesn't mean the storytelling itself was anything like that. Movement does not guarantee story content, it just defines pacing. You can't write pulp that moves at a snail's pace. You can write anything you want, as long as it constantly moves. The form isn't as limiting as the myths say.

However, a quick pace also means being straightforward and clear. The author is required to deliver on promises set up for the reader. Jarring passengers out of a moving rollercoaster car is fatal, as is tampering with their trust during a pulp tale. Keep the wheels on the track and inspect the machinery before you open for business. Know what the customer needs to have a good time.

You don't want to annoy your audience by trying to be clever or abrasive. You want the story to be as easy as possible to understand and digest for anyone who willingly picks it up. Give the majority of your readers what they desire.

Note that this doesn't mean dumbing down the story to appeal to a wider audience. Storytelling doesn't work that way. Appealing to the majority means writing something anyone can wrap their head around as long as they can read and want to engage in your genre. It requires being clear with your storytelling and not being wilfully obtuse.

Elevated language and purple prose are not entirely verboten, but both take a backseat to the story. Whatever the story itself needs to be as clear as possible is what you as the writer must do. Writers write and readers read, but readers can't do anything to make a writer's job harder. Therefore writers should not ask their readers to lift more than they can carry. Writers should keep their audience in mind when they write and always give them what they want. You are both on the same side, after all!

For example, there is the much beloved trope of starting a story in medias res. This means beginning your story in the middle of an action sequence and forcing the audience to connect to the story and characters by hoping they hook into your plot's events mid-action scene. This is a confusing way to begin a prose story. You are putting the heavy-lifting and burden on your reader to figure everything out on the very first page of the tale.

Do not do this, especially if you are beginning writer. You are treating your audience as if it is their duty to figure out why they should care about characters they don't know in situations they aren't yet invested in. You are asking for a tremendous level of trust from the reader that they have no reason to give you. A high barrier of entry has already been set up. Can you see how this is potentially fatal to your story?

Such a thing can work in a visual form like movies because the audience can get non-verbal visual clues, a winking soundtrack, and subtle performances from actors. There are multiple parts at play here that come together to make it work.

In prose form, you are limited with words and an audience that has to process all this new information through only one channel. It is information overload and demands too much of a reader who wishes to be eased into a story and learn why they should care about it. They cannot do so if the noise is too loud. It is not the reader's job to find a reason to keep reading your book.

If you can't show the reader how the conflict began without starting in medias res then it probably is not important to the plot and should be cut or altered. This narrative trick is too noisy and a distraction for a new reader trying to get interested in your story. Only keep what is necessary to the plot. Trim everything else lean.

Your story should begin as close to the action as possible without actually being immersed in it. The plot should begin as your character is close to walking into the situation that will turn their life upside down for the duration of the story. They can already be doing an activity that involves small action, such as a police officer on his way to a call, but any further forward and you risk throwing the audience into the deep end without knowing why they should care. Too early and you risk boring them. A balance between the two is needed. While pulp might be action focused, it still requires a deft touch to create.

An action story needs action, yes. That does not mean an action story needs to be drowned in car crashes, explosions, and knife fights, at every available moment. It means what occurs in between those exciting things is meaningful enough that it makes the action all the more engrossing when it happens. To make the moments count, the reader must be invested in the world the writer sets up. Ease them in with as little breathing room as possible, and then hit the gas until the tank runs out. This is a balancing act, but that is part of what makes pulp writing so exciting.

What it comes down to is that the secret to any action story is brevity. Things need to fly by at a good clip. Pulp writers of the past knew this and wrote hundreds to thousands of words to the effect back when these stories sold the most. They knew their audience, and they delivered what they wanted in spades.

Sure, you might say: that was then, and this is now. Audiences are different today, and, accordingly, they want something different. Certainly, we are in a much different place culturally from that time, so why should we look to the past for inspiration now? Surely, what worked back in the 1920s won't work today.

Believe it or not, people don't change that much. Interests are not so different now than they were a century ago. Audiences still love stories of good against evil, law against disorder, and adventures into the unknown, just as much as they did over a hundred years prior. Action writing is as beloved today as it was back in 1895. Audiences know what they love, and they always will. The only thing that changed was that the publishing industry back then provided it for them, and today they no longer do.

This is where NewPub comes in. The revolution in writing will come through a pulp focus.

To summarise: to be a pulp writer, you need to be an action writer. Your stories have to be about things happening, and happening at a good pace. You need to bring in the reader as quickly as possible while also easing them into your world, and you have to make sure each chapter ends with a good hook to bring them back for more. All this is part of the experience and is what makes pulp writing what it is.

Do you want to write pulp? If so, you must never forget about what you've learned here. This is one of the two biggest advantages you have over other forms of fiction. Action is a non-negotiable, and if you aren't writing action, then you aren't a pulp writer.

However, you might have noticed that there were two factors mentioned above. Certainly, we just covered the first, but what is the second advantage pulp has over everything else?

That would be the subject of the next chapter . . .

Whatever Happened to Wonder?

Creating action is only part the battle in writing a pulp story. It is an important piece of the pie, but it is only a large segment of it. The other half requires something else that has been forgotten by OldPub in their quest to reshape the literary landscape to the modern wasteland it has become. To be a pulp writer, you are required to supply your readers with wonder.

Wonder is an invaluable part to creating compelling fiction that is often overlooked these days. It is an aspect of creating that the industry has lost in the dark tangle of dinosaur publishing. This sensation of awe has long since been forgotten for stories of nihilistic sludge and sexual obsession. There is none of it to be had in OldPub, aside from very rare spurts.

What has replaced imagination and astonishment in modern writing has been stiff formula and tired subversion. Rigid rules that are required to be followed to the letter in order to be considered for publication are all that remains in OldPub. Creativity runs counter to the industry's goals. They have nothing to gain by teaching or encouraging upcoming writers to use their imagination. Hence their paid writing courses give it little focus. This is also why large chain bookstores all share the same outdated and bland genre classifications that haven't been relevant since the 1970s, if ever. They already have the industry they want—you simply need to accept it.

Sure, you'll come across checklists you need to fill in order to make it into an officially sanctioned genre. Professionals have an endless supply of rules for writing should you want them. Some circles might also have certain random quotas you need to hit in order to be accepted by the correct clique, but none of this is really very important. The wider audience doesn't care too much about genres or classifications, they only desire good stories.

They want to be wowed. OldPub doesn't understand that few people care how they get this mystical, intangible feeling—they just want it.

Choosing to be a pulp writer in the 21st century means working for wonder, the opposite of OldPub's antiquated ways. This is another advantage NewPub has over the Triassic industry. You can focus on what they cannot. This opens up an entire alternate marketplace without the interference of the zombies blocking your way forward.

This burgeoning market is invaluable for newer writers, because they are facing a hard road ahead of them. Thanks to shenanigans from OldPub over the decades, the pool of potential readers is smaller than it's ever been. They have sabotaged the entire pastime of reading and have made it uncool for kids.

Nobody reads anymore. This is universally agreed upon by both the literate and illiterate alike. Big book chains have closed because less and less customers are shopping there. Schools assign terrible slogs they designate as "important" books, thereby chasing children away from reading entirely, and at a time when reading has more competition than ever before in the form of video games, TV shows, podcasts, etc. All in all, the landscape for literature is not healthy; there are no shared traditions or agreed upon standards, and potential customers are wary of ever picking up a book—no matter how exciting it might look on the cover. Upcoming writers are at a severe disadvantage because of this disgusting sabotage that has gone back decades. Most normal Joes simply don't trust you.

For all intents and purposes, writing today is like flailing in the dark. Your chance of being discovered and landing on the New York Times Bestseller list is astronomically low to non-existent. The chances of most people you know even reading anything off of said list is even lower. That 20th century world just doesn't exist anymore. Readers are more fragmented than ever before, and you need to adjust your expectations accordingly.

The highest selling books not propped up by corporate-sponsored television and movie properties are all by authors who have been dead for decades. It's a small crowd of successful parties, and it's only shrinking. Room in the OldPub lifeboat doesn't allow for elbowroom, much less any advertising budgets for new writers.

But even if they did, it wouldn't matter. Mainstream audiences no longer trust those publishers. They haven't trusted them in ages.

When was the last time traditional publishing introduced a new writer that broke out big? Who was the last author who gained notoriety from someone other than your best friend who works at the library or local indie bookstore? When was the last time you saw a man on the street talking about hot new author X and how you just *must* read his new book? It doesn't happen anymore.

That hasn't been a reality in decades. If you're young enough, you might never have experienced it ever happening.

This is no small issue. Reading is now obscure. By all accounts, OldPub is flailing and utterly failing to draw in new customers or satisfying their shrinking pool of existing ones and is unable to offer anything fresh.

So what are they missing? They are missing that spark to draw readers in. Unless you like 400 page "realistic" thrillers or gritty pseudo-Tolkien tomes, there isn't anything out there for a new reader to sink their fangs into. And what actually is there is missing a very important factor to creating compelling fiction to draw those readers in.

The answer is simple: they have forgotten how to marvel the audience.

That might sound vague, and the notion of wonder often is these days, but back in the age of the pulps, long before the 1960s, this intangible sense of awe was the number one selling point for fiction. They didn't sell anyone on obtuse modern book covers or the same handful of corporate-approved genre ghettos. Pulps sold on the wow factor.

Simply look at the titles of the magazines from back in the day: *Astounding Stories*, *Weird Tales*, *Amazing Stories*, *Black Mask*, *Thrilling Adventures* . . . it goes on like this. Mundanity had no place in the pulps; they did everything big.

What was being sold was escapism to magical worlds where everything was larger than life, anything could happen, and genre boundaries weren't around to straightjacket the imagination of writers. Every magazine you picked up would transport you to an entirely different place. Restraint didn't exist.

Today, you are told by professionals what you are allowed and not allowed to write. Word count limits are stricter than ever before, and story content is run through content checkers. If you can't sum up your story in buzzwords based on irrelevant genres that big book stores erroneously rely on then no one in OldPub will give you a second glance. You also have to build your own newsletter subscribers and social media platform before the dinosaurs will take you under their wing. It's a lot of work the author has to do in order for OldPub to profit. The industry couldn't be any further from where it was half a century ago, and it changed so much in such a relatively short time.

The problem is the damage the industry has done to writing itself with their incessant rules. It isn't just about prose or plotting. It's not just about the action or tired "artsy" cover design. It isn't even about lack of creativity or stale formats like the 400-page realistic thriller paperback factory mainstream literature has become. OldPub has so formulized the act of writing that the medium no longer exists as a creative outlet, or for escapism, but as a set of boxes to check off to make sure it ends up in the correct hands of the right readers. It's purely about selling product to the approved demographics.

If a writer desires to sign a contract with OldPub, they are deciding to become a content creator to fill shelf space with product. They are not signing on to write creative and daring stories that only they can write for readers who want excitement. Writers in OldPub are just replaceable cogs in a rusted system, and that is exactly how they are treated by the top dogs.

But a writer can't write stories like that. You can't sit down and write a story specifically with the intent that it must do A, and include plenty of B, in order to be placed on an approved big chain bookseller new releases shelf. That is where creativity and spectacle go to die.

And, sure enough, OldPub is dying. Without wonder, they will never recover.

For an example, take what has become the modern Fantasy market. This post-pulp industry has largely abandoned every form of fantastical story that isn't either based on aping or subverting what J.R.R. Tolkien did decades ago. The idea that there was any other such tradition in the field has long been lost. The days of Lord Dunsany and *Weird Tales* are a distant memory, fading further with every passing day. It is now about the aesthetics and the image more than it is about what actually lies inside the cover.

Many authors and literature teachers hammer in that world-building is all one really needs to succeed in this small arena. You must write a long series of fat tomes that delve into the minutiae of everything in your concocted setting in order to truly suck your audience in and excite them. True wonder, they say, is about taking the reader to an alien world and exploring every bit of it in painstaking detail down to the mundane and irrelevant. This means readers should learn everything possible about this created universe, leaving little room for them to figure out anything for themselves. Unfortunately, this advice tends to drag newer writers down into an incessant cycle of world-building notes instead of ever writing an actual story. This path keeps them looking inward at themselves instead of outward at the audience awaiting their work. This isn't wonder.

The worst part of this advice is that it gets the appeal of Fantasy backwards. Fantastical worlds appeal because they are mysterious and foreign to the reader. The reader fills in the gaps themselves and uses their own brains to paint the edges of the picture while the writer concentrates on the core story. At least, that is how it once was. Authors are now told they need to explain everything in excruciating detail instead of letting their readers use their own imagination. The audience is now just meant to sit back and consume.

This is the complete opposite of how wonder works. The more you explain trivial details, and the more you focus on the mundanity of daily life, and the less imagination you allow your readers, the less they will be engaged. True wonder requires a deft touch, not a heavy slap. You need to allow the reader to use their own heads to fill in the gaps themselves.

Writing is all about allowing imagination to run free. If an artist is not inspiring awe then they are not an artist, but most likely a propagandist. That, or they have misunderstood what wonder is supposed to entail. Storytelling is meant to exercise the soul.

For one encapsulating example, take a random Lord Dunsany short story and then find any recent modern fantasy novel off a Barnes & Noble shelf and place them side by side. The differences are immediate and striking.

Dunsany's stories are rarely longer than a page, and he packs his short tales with wondrous sights, sounds, adventures, and ideas that leave the reader enthralled and possibly mystified at what they just experienced. Rarely are you left without at least some semblance of satisfaction from his tales, and you always leave looking back on what you've just read. He tells a complete series of events, does not spend much time at all on world building that isn't inferred, and leaves nothing hanging in the story except the reader's imagination. And these tales are less than a percent of the length of your average modern Fantasy book! This is a writer of pure imagination who respects his readers enough to use their heads.

In contrast, Modern Fantasy stories stretch on for near a thousand pages; they dig into minutia and world details that aren't very important to the plot, go deep into character histories and world politics, and parse out far too many sequels to get the entire tale, which usually ends up being some variation or play on the Lord of the Rings. The genre spends multiple books and years to finish a single story that doesn't contain half the weight or an eighth of the wonder of one single Lord Dunsany short.

How did these writers get to the complete opposite end of the spectrum from Dunsany, the man responsible for much of what they write? It is flabbergasting to see the differences a century can make.

This happens because new writers are told to focus on precisely the opposite thing they should be focusing on. As has been established, wonder is fiction's biggest strength, and new writers are taught to ignore it. This is how you get thousands of slight variations on the same book for near half a century. A lack of imagination this profound could only come from a classroom. Thankfully, no one needs to listen to these professors of cookie cutter moulds and dry ideas. NewPub no longer needs them.

What a writer needs to focus on, especially today, is on marveling the audience above all else. This requires rejecting everything they have been taught by those workshops and literature professors over the last few decades. It requires going back to basics, to when fiction sold the most and was truly inspiring and influential. Pulp is the cure to the modern industry's ills.

There is no wonder to a magic system. There is no wonder to nihilistic violence that ends with the least terrible person getting what they want. There is no wonder to a romance that is seen through a modern post-porn, sex-obsessive lens. There is no wonder to any story filtered through "reality", "content checkers", or hackneyed writer formulas that have been stale since the coked-out 1970s. In other words, there is no wonder to modern fiction.

This is why audiences have been fleeing from this sinking ship for decades while fanatics were too busy in their own little worlds to notice the boat was emptying. They were too enamored with making up new rules for writers to realize audiences weren't interested in what they were selling.

Of course, none this means that there are no rules to storytelling at all. There is in fact one rule an author must never break: internal consistency. Your story needs to be true to itself. As long as the rules you set up at the start of the tale are consistent throughout, the reader won't care what you do. It's really that simple.

Believe it or not, your audience is smart and will forgive just about anything you do as long as you fulfil the promise you set out with in the first sentence. They're a trusting bunch, and you owe them to fulfil that trust. Readers do this because they understand fiction better than most of the people who write it.

Readers read fiction because they want to escape. That is why it is called "fiction" to begin with, and why they are not reading non-fiction instead. If you are offering anything less than a world of pure imagination only limited by what you as a creator can dream up, you might as well just write a history book or a biography instead. Keep "realism" to non-fiction where it belongs.

Aside from the world-building, the other aspect of storytelling that is given too much focus is the main character: more specifically, a main character's "flaws" instead of their virtues. It is the regularly stated rule that the protagonist must be "interesting", broken, or in need of an arc, to be considered good. Otherwise, no one will read your story! But this is, again, the opposite of what the main character should be.

The protagonist is the link the reader has with your world. That connection should be crystal clear in order to maintain that channel between the two. Your main character must not be quirky, insane, or depraved. He must, in fact, be the most normal and moral person in your story. That doesn't mean he can't be a little off or have problems of his own, but he must be the best you've got to offer. There is a very simple reason for this that has been lost to literature courses and postmodern deconstruction nonsense: adventure stories should have a purity to them. This is how you maintain awe in the midst of action.

As has been discussed, when writing an adventure story or a weird tale, what matters most is the action. Anything that gets in the way of that, from world-building to unrelated relationship drama, takes something away from what is actually *happening* on the page. The noise dilutes and softens the impact. It is putting too many hats on and expecting the reader to hold them all for you.

In order to make sure the action is at the forefront, nothing else must stick out like a bad hangnail on the manicured hand of the story. This is why the protagonist needs to be crystal clear. He should not get in the way of the action itself and should serve to easily connect your reader into your story.

This focus on a normal main character also has a bonus effect on the plot and not one discussed much by writers, especially these days. With the obsession of "relatable" characters with "realistic" flaws, the one thing forgotten is that a damaged protagonist is not normal. Your audience will not get behind a lead character they cannot understand or want anything to do with. This is because your average person is not abnormal: they are normal, hence the definition of the word normal.

Ironically, by making your main character a normal good guy trying to do his best and being thwarted at every opportunity, you have created a "relatable" character. You did this without having to give them "faults" or "quirks" to distract from the main action. Your average reader is a normal person, too. They understand what it's like to be decent, not so much what it's like being a debauched loon. They can slide into the mindset of someone striving to do the right thing more than some jerk deciding who they should backstab or assault unprovoked.

To achieve maximum action and wonderment, a pulp tale's protagonist needs to be a decent human being. Otherwise, he will get in the way of the greater plot.

It must be said: this is not the same as writing a Mary Sue character. That tired character archetype has made a, largely unwelcome, return to OldPub fiction and Hollywood in recent years, but that hackneyed trope is not what is being discussed here.

Mary Sues are aberrations and mutations of normal heroes—they are not normal heroes themselves. They are a parody of good guy protagonists taken to cartoonish extremes. This is how they became such a punchline to begin with.

To write a Mary Sue, the character must do everything perfectly, be loved unconditionally by everyone (including enemies), be given everything just for being them, and not struggle too hard to achieve their goals. To anyone who has actually read a pulp story, it is easy to see the difference between the two. Those unfamiliar with pulp heroes confuse the two regularly to the regret of anyone who has actually glanced at even a single classic tale. Pulp heroes work very hard to achieve their goals against villains who detest them and make their quest a veritable gauntlet of betrayals and ambushes. They are the very opposite of Mary Sue protagonists.

The truth is that Mary Sues do not exist in the pulps. There are no pulp characters that fall into this category despite all of them being normal characters with no major personal vices aside from typical failings such as not being athletic or being ignorant in a scientific field. They may be the best humanity has to offer, but they work for everything they have. Their enemies loathe them; they stumble on their way to thwarting the villain; and they earn their victory through skills and knowledge they acquired along the way and do so with their equally-impressive allies. They are not handed anything just for being special. Pulp heroes are not Mary Sues; Mary Sues are parodic inversions of pulp heroes.

This goes to show why the villains in pulp stories were the complete opposite of the hero. Where the protagonist represented the best in humanity, the antagonist represented the worst. Horror writers would know this better than anyone. The antagonist must represent the opposite of what the protagonist is, both in goals and in general characterization. This makes the threat stand out all the more and makes it as threatening as possible. This dynamic difference between both protagonist and antagonist allows both to stand out from each other without diluting the action. It makes the story sharper.

In a short pulp story where every word counts, getting to the point is paramount. In order to make the characters clash and differentiate without having to waste time in prose, pulp writers did the most obvious thing they could do. They made their rivals be complete opposites.

This provides a sharp black and white divide and allows the reader to concentrate on what matters most: the story. Wonder is a key ingredient to hooking readers into pulp fiction, but you need the audience tied to the stakes for it to be as effective as possible. Black and white morality provides the heavy-lifting of investment for the audience without sacrificing on pacing or movement. It's straightforward, and that's why it works and was used for so very long.

If you ever wanted to know why pulp stories focused on "simplistic" morality and "black and white" characters, this is why. The writers assumed the audience understood what is good and what is evil and worked on those assumptions to create stories the readers can get behind with as low a barrier to entry as possible. Modern "complex" characters take away from this sharp storytelling and needlessly divide audiences while having to slowly set everything up in a new moral framework.

That simply isn't how pulp writing works. The longer you take to set it up, the further it gets away from being pulp. It detracts from both the sense of wonder and the action.

The wonder comes from the action, not the characters. The characters are there to drive the plot; the plot is not there to babysit the characters. Everything in a story has its place, which is why this simple formula worked so well.

This is essentially the exact opposite of what has been taught in writing courses for decades. They say you need to linger on characters at the expense of outward action. But writing pulp means writing outward, not inward. This is why pulp is considered passé and has been locked outside of the OldPub asylum.

How does the protagonist's world treat those zombie dragons he mentioned offhand in one passage about wildlife? Where is the heroine's home world that she wants to return to so badly, and is it really the paradise she says it is? Where were those plasma guns manufactured? Who forged the fire sword? Did the antagonist really come from the Soviet Bloc, or is that a cover for an even darker past? These are all questions that wouldn't affect the main plot, and are ones the readers are better left to mull on their own.

That is wonder: leaving the reader with bits to chew on that they can either take or leave, or put their own spin on. This exercise of imagination gets them more involved in the story. Pulp writing does this all while keeping the story on a tight leash.

The old pulp writers also concentrated on getting to the point. Every story they wrote was as short as it needed to be. No fluff, no fat, and no flab. Sharp writing, focused on action from word one up to the conclusion, was all that mattered. Because of this sharpness, it allowed the reader's mind to run wild with possibilities. This is the reason pulp stories were strict on form.

The magazine format aided in keeping writers in check, too. You could have stories of any length in their pages, even things such as poems. There was no limit in creativity, despite the straightforward framework these magazines emphasized. This is essentially why those older stories had far more punch than newer ones do. They had more legroom to do anything they wanted.

This limited space also meant the language had to be focused on the story. This didn't mean forgoing poetic language, or even purple prose, but it had to be centered on the events of the plot at hand. Every word was required to contribute to painting the exact picture the reader needed in order to get the gist of what was happening, nothing more or less. After all, pretty language means nothing if it is not in service of anything the reader cares about. The words you write are meant to work for the audience, not your ego. Sharpness is everything, and the masters knew this!

At this point, you might be asking just where this intangible idea of the astonishing actually comes from. These pulps looked like they had a lot of limits, so where is that sense of wonder? How can you use your imagination with so many rules on what you shouldn't do? If the sensation is not in the world-building, if it's not in the characters, and it's not in flowery language, then where is it? It surely can't just be in the action! After all, how much spectacle is there in shooting a villain and getting the girl? That's hard to swallow.

The answer to those questions might surprise you: the wonder is in all of those above elements at once.

When you write a story centered on the action, the plot naturally follows a chain of events as tightly as possible from the beginning to the end. As a consequence, this opens up questions in between these developments. Since the audience doesn't see everything and are only given a taste of the surrounding world, this adds natural mystery to the tale. It is the same with character motivations and backgrounds—because they are not a focus and are not on stage it naturally makes the reader curious about them. The sharper writing of pulp can use evocative language to add some flavor, but because it remains hinged on the plot, the reader's own thoughts can come to conclusions themselves.

The audience is tasked with the only thing a writer should ever make them do: they have to use their imagination. Writers should never spoon-feed everything to their readers, and this is why. You can't take away the opportunity for readers to use their imagination both for their benefit, and yours.

Smaller and sharper stories are able to offer this ephemeral quality in a way longer stories can't. They allow the reader to explore a vast world in a shorter length, as opposed to the modern obsession of exploring a tiny world in a vast length. Pulp writing allows more brain-bending thoughts than longer works do and that is why it was so successful.

You need that sense of astonishment around the action. This "Sense of Wonder" is the main ingredient in any fiction that relies on adventure or the fantastical. You need to instill as much excitement in your readers as is possible to move them.

The issue is that many post-pulp authors have made it their goal to bolt down the more freewheeling aspects of their imagination to a sort of Secular Bible of what can and cannot be done in fiction. Much of this is because of the bookstore-obsessed genre ghetto that organizes and files every book in neat categories, and coloring outside the lines to prevent easy classification is frowned upon. The reason newer authors think this way is due to advice from self-appointed experts that other self-appointed experts put in charge of their industry long before these newer writers were born. More and more rules were made up over time that had nothing to do with the roots of storytelling and ended up diluting and sanding off the edges to the fiction world. This was one of the first casualties to fiction after the pulp era, and it has been relegated as unimportant for ages now.

Looking back now, it is clear that this was a terrible move. The truth is that you can do anything in a story simply by focusing on marveling the audience. This is an author's most reliable trump card. You can draw from the world you live in and your imaginative ideas of what another place might be like. We live in an incredible, infinite universe. We were made to think big. You have no limitations other than what you impose upon yourself, or what you let others enforce on you.

Pulp writing is the emphasis on big over small, and it does this by focusing on the small before the big. Writers do more by focusing on less. This is what the Pulp Mindset is all about.

The goal of writing fiction is to bring out imagination. Imagination is built on marveling over the universe. No one can imagine the sort of things you can, which means as a writer, you are already holding cards in your hand that no one else at the table has. You don't need a prose-writing gimmick, or tacky image, or convoluted genre tag, in order to stand out, no matter what the writer's workshop industry tells you.

While the old publishing industry fumbles through failing formulas and trying to figure out just why so many readers have abandoned them, you have the advantage. They might have forgotten the path to wonder, to spectacle itself. But not you—you have the power of pulp writing to light the way forward. You now have what they have long abandoned.

Should you take only one thing from this chapter with you, make it be this: there are millions of undiscovered worlds and possibilities out there in the universe waiting to be found. Whether through untold horrors, fantastical sights, miracles, or scientific breakthroughs, it all means the same thing in the end.

The only limit is your imagination.

Revolution Writing

Change is coming, and every new writer will need to be prepared. Most writers still aren't ready, worshiping institutions and methods that have harmed their medium, but they will soon be thrown headfirst into this new world, whether they like it or not. The revolution in writing is going to come from you. Before moving forward, it is time to recap some of what you have learned.

NewPub is a term that obviously infers something fresh, different from the norm. OldPub is ancient and has already been left behind. That ice age industry itself has been on a downhill slide for decades, locking writers into checkbox mindsets as audiences turned away for less constrictive mediums. OldPub has already stumbled their way into defeat. They will never recover what they have lost. But you now know this.

Think about the last time one of the Big Five book publishers put out a new high selling author that got everyone talking. This isn't referring to your Aunt Mabel who hangs out with the other ladies at the book club, but your Uncle Art who prefers watching the History Channel to reading. Has anyone at your workplace or at your school randomly brought up a high-selling author whose new work is just absolutely jaw dropping and downright inspiring? Judging by what sells right now, which isn't much, it is highly doubtful. There is little chance they are reading anything from OldPub that isn't old books being repackaged and resold with worse covers.

The industry is out of touch. The reason they are called OldPub is because they are incapable of creating anything new that resonates with audiences. They can only rely on old product to make their money.

You have the advantage of being in a fresh place with an edge they do not. You have tools, options, and the means, to put out what they cannot. You now have a pulp mindset, and the wide open playing field of

NewPub.

With the endless frontier of online publishing, you could theoretically put out anything you want, at any point. Nothing is really stopping you, aside from your own skill. Whether a short story, novelette, or novella, you can even release stories at any length you so desire, unlike the old guard. No more folding and morphing stories to fit in OldPub's approved boxes.

That said, just because you can do it doesn't mean you should. There are two tasks you need to accomplish before publishing anything online: getting cover art and acquiring professional editing. No writer can skimp on either of these two.

Unless you yourself are a master artist, photographer, or photo manipulator, you will need to hire an artist to create your book cover. There is no getting around it. If you want to be taken seriously, you need to present yourself as professional as possible.

Look at your favorite covers and hire an artist to create one for you in that style. Make your cover the best it can be. There is no shortage of talented artists that can give you a product just as good, if not better, than what OldPub puts out. And they are guaranteed to charge more reasonable prices, too.

The second thing you need is an editor. This can't be avoided. You need a second set of eyes to look at your draft as deeply as you do.

This is the one thing a writer cannot go without, regardless of how good they get, unlike cover design. Even if you are an editor yourself, you will need to hire one to help you. No matter how much of a great writer you feel you are, you will miss serious errors. A writer is always too immersed in their own story to fully see all angles on their work. It's an inevitable blind spot, and no writer can avoid it or learn to overcome this reality. They need a neutral third party to find the issues they would otherwise not even notice. Editors exist for this very important task, and every single writer needs one. No exceptions.

Most everything an author does is for the benefit of their audience, and this used to be championed a lot more than it is today. As you are now well aware, the real revolution in NewPub is going to be the influx of writers who are interested in giving readers what they want. This is why you need professional art and cover design to truly dazzle them. It is going to be this audience-first mentality that makes the difference over OldPub.

This bears repeating: your story needs to be aimed at the highest amount of people that are interested in the stories you plan to write. This requires writing adventure stories for every sort of person who might be interested in an adventure story. It is not smart to attempt appealing to a fringe segment of a demographic. You are limiting potential success by trying for a cult hit. Those things happen naturally.

This all might sound like a lot, to aim high and broad, but it's really not—as long as you give your audience an honest to goodness adventure, the majority of readers will come along for the ride. Believe it or not, audiences don't demand writers reinvent the wheel with every single story they write. They just want a complete moral tale full of astonishment and excitement that they can engage in. This is what every writer owes their reader.

This next revolution will anger some, but it is an elephant that needs to be addressed. Writers are going to have to bring back the morality of good storytelling. No more sludge, nihilism, and emptiness. The obsession with subversion in OldPub has chased readers away—the focus on clear morality will bring them to NewPub. Your audience is comprised of normal people who like good and hate evil. Give them a story that reflects that.

It's been established that both a sense of awe and action are paramount to creating a story to satisfy, but it also requires knowing what readers want on a deeper level. A majority of readers desire a story where good is good, evil is evil, justice is expected, and issues are resolved and put right (in some fashion) by the end. They want a world set right. The trick to this is about presenting morals every reader believes in on some level. This is a controversial notion, but that is what audiences long for and what every pulp writer knew. They managed it, and so can you.

However, the audience does not desire flat tales, ones where every character preaches a unifying message throughout. Moral stories are those where every major character aspires to be the best they can be. The second one is not propaganda; it's just being honest. Everyone wants to read stories of characters striving to be better and improve their situation. If they desired less, then they wouldn't be reading escapist entertainment to begin with.

This is why you need to give the audience what they want, in the most basic sense. They long for the good and the true. You need to appeal to the majority of potential readers, and think they are worth writing for, in order to get to this stage. That is the beating heart of pulp writing.

Now, this is controversial advice, and has been seen as such since the 1960s, but it is the correct path. The concept of writing a moral story, never mind for as many readers as possible, is seen as being either impossible or arrogant on the part of the author. However, it's not.

Morality is used as a curse word these days, after decades of OldPub propaganda asserting that putting morals in a story is preaching, but that is only if the writer is bad at writing. Morality is a storytelling tool every bit as invaluable as spectacle or action, yet neglected and forgotten to the extent that most potential readers have walked away due to being preached at. The lack of proper morality in modern writing is a major reason why there are fewer readers than ever before. Readers need something to believe in and root for. This focus on the moral and good sounds controversial, but it really isn't once you get down to it.

A moral story simply means a story that has a clear point any reader can understand and put their weight behind. A prince sets out to rescue the princess and does so. A villain causes a problem, and the hero fixes it. A monster terrorizes a town, and the town stops it. The moral thing is putting order to disorder. Readers understand the stakes subconsciously, and they know what it takes to put right. They want the hero to win, and the villain to fail.

A moral writer completes the initial goal promised at the beginning of their story. Whether it happens in a strange and off-kilter way is up to the author—but it must happen. Denying the audience their payoff is subversion of the worst sort, and, while a small group of modern readers may claim that this is what they want, the wider audience will never put up with it. This is because subversive writing is antithetical to being pulp, which is audience first, and is instead out to upturn the reader's world. Subversion is the author putting his own ego before the audience to try and flip their thinking. It works against the audience and seeks to combat them. This is an anti-reader mindset. Readers do not pay you money so you can spit at them.

It is not up to the writer to try and warp the way the reader thinks. This is an arrogant, writer-first mentality that thinks the audience lesser than they are. The author caters to the reader: doing this the wrong way is what chases the audience away. Readers can do without you: you cannot do without readers.

Subversion is treated as a synonym for good, and it is anything but. It can be used as a tool every now and then to mix things up, but too many writers lean on it as an escape hatch for their mediocre story. Nonsensical and limp twists and unsatisfying payoffs are hallmarks of modern subversive storytelling. This overdone technique is all over OldPub and Hollywood, and audiences are fleeing from them in droves. The last thing reading needs is less readers. Stop relying on subversion to tell your stories.

Subversive writing has become so prominent in recent years that it has become easy to forget just why it is so shallow, and why older generations didn't need to use it. This incessant table-flipping formula persists in spite of how audiences have become more and more vocal in their hatred of it. At some point, authors need to listen to their audience and abandon this style of writing. Readers have had enough; so start writing normal stories again.

Here is a comparison to help show the difference between straightforward plotting and subversive plotting.

Normal plotting

- Hero is shot
- Hero goes out for revenge
- Events transpire to make his goal difficult
- Hero takes his revenge
- The end

Subversive plotting

- Hero is shot
- Hero goes out for revenge
- *TWIST* Villain is justified in killing hero
- Hero dies and villain gets away
- The end

Do you see the difference? The first is a straightforward revenge plot that has been written to tremendous success thousands of times over a countless number of years. It works because the setup is straightforward and clear, and it can lead to any sort of plot deviation before it wraps up at the climax where justice is dispensed. You can do anything you want along the way, as long as it logically follows on from what came before. What really matters is where it all ends up. This is what readers want: a striking setup leading to a satisfying pay off.

What a subversive story does is not allow the promised payoff to happen because the writer believes he is too clever to give the audience what they want. The subversive writer then believes he can create an ending surpassing the logical conclusion the story was headed towards. He does this by tricking his audience. He believes he can outdo the audience's expectations and wants by creating something wholly original no one has ever seen before in the entire medium.

But he can't. Every story progresses in a natural fashion. All a reader wants is that promised conclusion, which follows on from the first sentence of the story that continues on until they reach the last one. As a writer, you owe them this.

For instance, take the earlier revenge story plot. Now say the villain is actually justified in trying to kill the protagonist at the beginning, and the hero is actually not worthy of his revenge. But we don't learn this crucial piece of information until a plot convenient twist takes place to shatter the audience's illusions late in the story. The villain is actually good! This is an attempt to fool the reader into liking a character they don't want to like, not an attempt to entertain them with a revenge story. So the hero does not get his revenge, and the villain gets no punishment because he doesn't deserve any. The entire story was for nothing.

You see, subversive writers believe this is okay because "all people are trash" and "nothing means anything", so the lesson the writer wants to teach takes precedent over a satisfying fulfillment of the plot. It is a way of forcing a lesson into the story over letting the more universal moral that comes pre-packaged in such a tale run free. True moral stories do not have to beat their message on the heads of the audience, because they are natural and obvious to everyone.

These days, it is more revolutionary to give the customer what they want instead of assuming you can give them something better. What they want out of you is a unique way to get to the satisfying payoff—not a way to subvert the payoff itself. This difference is far more important than you might think. Audiences might not always know what they want, but they know what they need.

And to cut a canard off at the knees: a plot twist is not subversion.

To use the above revenge plot, say the villain the hero is searching for turns out to be the best friend that helped him along the way the whole time, and now the two must confront each other. That is a twist, but it is not subversion. The antagonist is still the antagonist, and the hero is still the hero. It is still delivering the fulfilment of a revenge tale the opening of the story promised. The plot was not rendered meaningless by this reveal, and it adds a wrinkle into the proceedings. The core of the story is not warped, and the audience still gets a payoff. If there is any area where the writer should be free to do whatever they want, it should not be in neglecting to fulfill promises to the audience. This is a non-negotiable.

If anything, the freedom in writing should come from smashing modern genre ghettos. Your storytelling should not be limited by relatively recent inventions such as outdated genre categorizations. That is where the real revolution should be.

You might think it strange to champion traditional storytelling but not traditional genre boundaries; however, that comes packaged with the incorrect notion that those classical genre boundaries are classical at all. They are not. They were in fact created within the last century, after the pulps died out, and were used to stock shelves in big chain bookstores. These categories no longer apply today, if they ever did to begin with. They were invented by OldPub, and OldPub is on the way out.

There were no science fiction or fantasy stories in the pulps. Everything was an adventure, a weird tale, a mystery, or a romance. Sometimes descriptors such as "super science" or "space opera" would be used, but they weren't considered genres as they are today. It was an entirely different literary world in the first half on the 20th century, and much more freeing than what it came to be in the second half.

Most people do not subscribe to OldPub's categories. Tell them you're writing a hard science fiction novel, and they'll look at you blankly. Tell them you're writing an adventure story about shrinking aliens down to the size of atoms to do battle in a microscopic kingdom beyond the naked eye, and suddenly their interest piques. They might both be correct descriptions of the story, but only the second really means anything to a passerby. You already understand that the audience wants wonder, but readers don't care where they get it from or what the label is.

The pulps knew this, and they cashed in on it. NewPub knows this, too, and are poised to offer that same experience to readers.

As an example, here is a reminder of the titles of some of the most popular and enduring pulp magazines of the period:

- *All-Story*
- *Wonder Stories*
- *Weird Tales*
- *Amazing Stories*
- *Adventure*
- *Black Mask*
- *Short Stories*
- *Argosy*
- *Amazing Stories*
- *Planet Stories*

The pattern is pretty obvious. The stories inside were what was being sold in those magazines, and they were being advertised on something other than modern genre tropes.

You get the hint at the type of stories that will be included inside without being explicitly beat over the head with cobbled together buzzwords and slogans. You want to feel astonished and amazed? Then pick up an issue!

What's more is that none of the magazines above tended to run the same sort of stories as the others did. You could have dragons, super science, blood demons, hard boiled heroes, and biplane dogfights, all in the same story, and without the modern wink such stories would have today. In an OldPub bookstore, these would have each been shelved in different corners of the store.

Modern genre ghettos cannot contain the sort of wild stories the magazines unleashed on their masses of eager readers. They appealed to anyone with this approach, from children to teens and to adults. The pulps did everything, and they went everywhere.

There were boxing stories, train stories, airplane stories, undersea stories, sports stories . . . sometimes writers even mashed these up in the same tale. This doesn't happen in the stale atmosphere of OldPub. There is a wide world of adventure that audiences are hungry for. All you need do is have a pulp mindset, and you can achieve it, too.

And that mindset used to be far more prevalent than it is now. The loss of this imagination and action first mentality has led to the destruction of many beloved properties that were created under a pulp influence. From space operas to action movies, the heart of adventure has been crushed to dust. So much was so easily lost and forgotten over a mere century, and it puzzling as to how it happened to fast.

But the first step is admitting the problem exists. Now it can be corrected.

Video games, adventure and horror movies, animation, tabletop games like Dungeons & Dragons, comic books, manga, anime, *bande dessinee*, metal music, and just about anything you can imagine in the entertainment world has its roots in the pulps. This influence is what inspired and caused them to grow to be such monsters in the pop culture of the 20th century. There are few things from that time span that had as much influence as the pulps did, and that should never be forgotten again. If they were good enough to inspire those things that came later and were good enough for the audience, then it is good enough for you now as a writer. Return to tradition.

The real revolution is not only realizing this loss of the pulp mindset but making up for it. Reclaim what was lost. The pulp mindset at its core is summed up in this truth: give the audience what they want.

This should be easy since you now know what they want. What they want is pulp, and giving them that pulp, unfiltered and untainted, is how you will succeed.

Rev it Up & Go!

NewPub is reality now. The 20th Century is over, and it is not coming back. Many have used this passage of time as an argument for burying the pulps, tarring them, and rewriting them to remove "problematic" elements from their histories. After all, "times have changed," which means we must change with them.

Yes, the pulps are gone, but there is still much they can teach us. Just as when a grandparent dies yet one takes their advice forward with them, so must the same be done with art. The pulps were the most popular literature of the 20th Century, and their influence has been deliberately scrubbed from popular entertainment by a creaking industry that is nearing its ugly end. For those who slander the pulps as outdated are desperately holding on to OldPub, and OldPub is a meandering zombie not long for this world. Unlike the pulps, there is nothing to take forward from them.

The future ahead of you is going to be rocky, and you won't have much in the way of a support system for a while, but with the right mindset, you will be able to traverse this minefield with far greater peace of mind. Effort can take you far.

All that is left is to rev up the engine and start the car. All the tips and tricks in the world aren't going to matter if they aren't applied to the work in question. It's time to pull out onto the road and drive.

Now, after reading this book, you have everything you need to get into the pulp mindset and become the writer you need to be. Being a pulp writer is about doing, and that is all that remains for you to succeed. Go out and do it! You have all the tools, you have the ambition, and you have the right mindset. What more do you need?

This book was only ever meant to be a guide on learning the mindset needed to tackle the world of NewPub rising up around you. As OldPub dies, writers are going to have to change everything they know and that includes abandoning the paths that lead to nowhere. There are many truths new writers need to learn, and they simply aren't learning them—because no one will tell them. But now you know what they will learn later the hard way.

The truth is that OldPub's decrepit ways will not help you anymore. They have nothing to offer upcoming writers.

You are not going to get a multi-million dollar contract from a big publisher—that era is over. You can get steady results by working on your own to achieve more independently. You can do this by finding readers that the dying industry has forgotten and abandoned. You can write anything, and you can reach anyone: you don't need to rely on the blessings of an agent or an out-of-touch corporation to give you that chance. All it takes is plenty of practice and effort on your part.

There is a whole industry out there that exists simply to help new writers flourish outside the OldPub system. This is how badly the Big Five have failed. Now, you have no excuse to avoid facing the new world springing up around you. There are plenty of ways to move forward in the burgeoning publishing sphere.

As for other works in this area worth reading, there are a few worth mentioning.

Should you want tips on improving your actual writing, there are some books that can help you along the way.

Bryce Beattie's *Pulp Era Writing Tips* will help you understand the thought process of some of the masters. His work contains essays and articles from those written during the days of the pulps. Get it straight from the horse's mouth in this one.

Author and critic Tom Simon has written three books on the magic inherent in writing and storytelling. These works are filled with essays that will allow you to see and understand writing from a far different angle than what is taught in writer workshops. The three books are called *Style is the Rocket, Death Carries a Camcorder,* and *Writing Down the Dragon,* and all come highly recommended.

A list of non-fiction books in this category to avoid would be much longer. Unless you are looking for tips on writing or inspiration, be wary of books written by agents or writers of the old system. Much of what they will tell you is what OldPub wants, not what readers actually desire. There are some good ones but use your discretion when reading.

Also avoid any writing book made to fashion novels in the image of screenplays: pulp isn't meant to be written like a film. You are writing books, and your stories should not be bent to fit other mediums or vice versa. Stick to non-fiction works by other authors that strike your fancy to give you writing tips.

If you wish to learn more about the pulps themselves there is author Ron Goulart's *Cheap Thrills* that gives a brief but illuminating look on the pulp era. He even interviews some of the people who were there at the time from authors to experts.

There isn't any other book in the field on the pulps that comes close to his on the subject.

For something more specialized, Jeffro Johnson's *Appendix N: A Literary History of Dungeons & Dragons* comes highly recommended. The author describes the legendarily influential tabletop game and its relationship to the pulps that inspired its existence. There, you can see just how much these silly books influenced what you love.

In those above works, you can see just what a pulp mindset can do for those who believe in it. Find what interests you and give it a go. All of them come highly recommended.

This is the key to moving forward in a stagnating and bloodless publishing world. Sometimes, going back is the only way to move forward. Should you wish to go beyond the death of the old publishing world, you will need to do the same.

What better way to throw off the chains of OldPub then by embracing what they threw away indiscriminately? Pick up what they left behind in their mad dash for irrelevancy and use it as a tool in your own journey as a writer.

New publishing is here. You can find thousands of authors, readers, and artists, out there embracing this bright frontier. Everything has changed, and it will never return to the way it once was. OldPub will bite, kick, and thrash, as they drift out into the water, but they will still drown regardless. You don't need them anymore, and neither do readers. NewPub is here to stay.

You are now a part of this new system, and your learned pulp mindset will be what allows you adapt to this strange land before you—a world of imagination, danger, action, and fun. Go beyond the sky and find whatever limit you can far above the dark clouds.

No one can stop you now.

You have the tools, the mindset, and the means. All you need to do is apply them. Now, it is time to create!

There's nothing left to say except welcome aboard. OldPub is dead, long live NewPub. The 21st Century is finally here.

Welcome to the revolution.

About the Author

JD Cowan is a writer with an obsession for stories and Truth. He takes pleasure in looking for Light in the places where darkness grips the tightest. His works include "Someone is Aiming for You & Other Adventures", "Gemini Warrior" for Silver Empire, and short stories in Storyhack, the PulpRev Sampler, and the Planetary Anthology Series. His works can found at Amazon.

He blogs at wastelandandsky.blogspot.ca and can be found on Twitter @wastelandJD for those interested.

JD's Works

Knights of the End
Grey Cat Blues
Gemini Warrior
Someone is Aiming for You & Other Adventures
The Pulp Mindset: A NewPub Survival Guide
Gemini Drifter *[Coming Soon!]*
Brutal Dreams *[Coming Soon!]*

Made in the USA
Middletown, DE
31 January 2022

60125032R00045